WORKING WITH GROUPS
FROM
DYSFUNCTIONAL
FAMILIES

VOLUME 1

WORKING WITH GROUPS FROM DYSFUNCTIONAL FAMILIES

STRUCTURED EXERCISES IN HEALING

VOLUME 1

CHERYL HETHERINGTON

WHOLE PERSON ASSOCIATES
210 W Michigan
Duluth MN 55802-1908
800-247-6789

WHOLE PERSON ASSOCIATES
210 W Michigan
Duluth MN 55802 - 1908
218-727-0500

Barbara Sunderland Smith, M.O.C., provided invaluable help in improving the organization, creativity, and clarity of this book. An expert at recognizing the elements, she gently rearranges them with a velvet hammer/pen.

For information on Cheryl Hetherington's lecture and workshop schedule, please send a stamped self-addressed envelope to:

Hetherington & Associates
PO Box 367
Iowa City, IA 52244
(319) 337-9461

Also by Dr. Cheryl Hetherington
Bringing Your Self To Life: Changing Co-Dependent Patterns

CONTENTS

INTRODUCTION

In an ideal world, families would always provide a sheltering environment where the members could grow and learn to love. The family would offer unconditional love, respect, and acceptance. Even when its members made mistakes, they would know that their families loved them and would forgive them. There would be few secrets. There would be room to change and become independent with differing opinions and attitudes. Each member would be allowed to develop an individual identity, and emotional intimacy would be a family norm.

In the real world, families are made up of flawed individuals who don't or can't always give what is needed. These imperfect families may be dysfunctional revolving around a person, usually a parent, whose personal traits dictate the entire style of the family. The dysfunctional situation— a very rigid or controlling parent, an alcoholic or abusive parent, or a mentally or physically ill family member—forces the rest of the family to pay more attention to the needs of the central figure than to their own wishes, needs, and feelings.

In a dysfunctional family, members try to keep the peace by "walking on eggshells" and being excessively concerned with everyone around them. They fail to develop a sense of self, and never learn who they really are. In order to heal, people from dysfunctional families need to look inward and find themselves as the first step toward finding peace.

If members of dysfunctional families have spent their entire lives worrying about concerns of others at their own expense, how do they learn to start taking care of their own inner needs? Group work is a powerful healing tool that can help people identify their pain and the patterns that cause it. By working with a group, they can begin to change the patterns learned in their dysfunctional families.

HOW TO USE THE EXERCISES

The 29 exercises in this book provide step-by-step instructions for group and individual healing processes. The facilitator can use the exercises as part of a flexible format, depending on the situation. For example, each exercise can be used as the focus of a session for a group that meets 29 times, or specific exercises can be selected for a group that meets only once. The exercises can also be combined into workshops and classes.

The facilitator can increase the power of the exercises by alternating them with other activities, such as lectures and discussions. One valuable activity for groups is to show videotaped segments of movies or television shows that demonstrate oppressive family rules or dysfunctional interactions. Some of these videotapes may be funny—for example, most Woody Allen films and many TV situation comedies portray dysfunctional families. It's important to laugh; humor is an important part of the healing process. When group members can talk and laugh about their own patterns and struggles with recovery, they become more open to change.

Whatever exercises and materials are used, it is necessary to take time for participants to integrate the information. Everyone has unique experiences, and they need time to process the exercises, videotapes or other activities in light of their own family backgrounds.

Although each exercise in this book is unique, all are designed to provide a mirror for participants to aid in exploration of feelings from the past and present. Participants uncover painful, and sometimes joyful, feelings. The facilitator must provide both structured-group and individual time, such as writing or fantasizing, so that participants can experience the feelings both with others and by themselves.

Many of the exercises require separating participants into small groups. In most cases it's best to use some random method, for forming these subgroups, rather than allowing people to self-select into groups of friends or acquaintances. Some effective sorting methods are counting off, or dividing groups according to the color of clothing they are wearing or their birth month.

THE SEQUENTIAL PROCESS OF HEALING

Each section of this book organizes exercises according to a special focus, based on the step-by-step process of healing. The sections are: **Taking Stock, Journaling,** and **Healing Patterns**.

The **Taking Stock** section promotes self-knowledge. Shared experiences and spoken secrets help participants realize that others have feelings similar to their own. This can help to build trust, and is a way to get honest feedback.

People from dysfunctional families typically learn to put others first, to ignore their own feelings, to be perfect, to keep secrets, to behave compulsively, and to over-extend themselves. They're always looking outward, so they have very little self-knowledge. The exercises in this section help participants become more aware of their hidden feelings and patterns. Each exercise provides a format for developing a new understanding of those denied, forgotten or unknown parts of self.

The exercises may bring up feelings that surprise or frighten participants. Allow time for feelings to be expressed or validated. Provide quiet time and breaks where people can talk or be by themselves.

The **Journaling** section includes exercises that help people acknowledge their current feelings, something often avoided or denied by people from dysfunctional families. Writing down their inner thoughts provides a safe and private way to explore feelings and experiences.

Many people from dysfunctional families learn to be "on," to perform for an unseen audience much of the time. They are not used to being quiet and looking inward. The exercises in this section encourage participants to explore their feelings more deeply, and then to share these newly-discovered parts of themselves with others.

Although the exercises involve small-group discussion, assure participants that they should share only what feels safe for them. Group interaction helps participants to learn something about themselves, and to realize that others have similar feelings.

The **Healing Patterns** section includes exercises that help people repattern relationships, first in the group and then in the real world. Coping in a dysfunctional family usually involves rigid rules and ineffective communication so new skills must be learned to overcome these patterns. The exercises in this section help participants adjust and change their behavior to decrease dysfunctional behavior.

Many people from dysfunctional families grow up too quickly, taking on adult responsibilities far too early. The playful childlike parts of themselves got squelched and left behind. Some of the exercises in this section involve reclaiming those valuable childlike feelings and characteristics.

THE FORMAT

The format of *Working with Groups from Dysfunctional Families* is designed for easy use. You'll find that each exercise is described completely, including: goals, group size, time frame, materials needed, step-by-step process instructions, and variations.

☞ *Special instructions for the trainer and scripts to be read to the group are typed in italics.*

✔ Questions to ask the group are preceded by a check.

➤ Directions for group activities are indicated by an arrow.

● Mini-lecture notes are preceded by a bullet.

RESOURCES FOR THE FACILITATOR

The structure of the exercises as they are prescribed in the resource assumes that the facilitator has already developed the basic skills as a group leader and listener, and is knowledgeable about dysfunctional family dynamics. The books listed in Section 5, Resources, offer more information about the interpersonal dynamics of people from dysfunctional families. These resources can help the facilitator fine-tune skills and gain information.

The facilitator should become clear about his or her own issues before leading groups through these exercises. Do not use the groups for working out personal issues of the facilitator!

Throughout the book, the gender pronouns he, she, him, her, etc. are used randomly, without implications in any specific case. This method is used to make the book more readable without the disruptive use of he/she or her/him.

While these exercises have already been thoroughly field-tested, they are also meant to prod your creativity. So, go ahead, experiment and enjoy!

Cheryl Hetherington
1994

DEFINITIONS OF TERMS

Boundaries: Physical or emotional limits that mark your personal territory or sense of self. A boundary may signify a number of things; what you are and are not willing to do; what you are and are not willing to be. Boundaries may apply to your body, your mind, your emotions, your spirits, or your rights.

Dysfunctional family: A family whose behavior is dictated by a central figure or situation, such as alcoholism, abuse, or mental or physical illness. In a dysfunctional family, feelings are avoided and denied. Family members tip-toe around the central figure or figures, unaware of and/or unable to express their feelings, wishes, or opinions without emotional or physical oppression.

Guilt: A constant feeling that you made a mistake. The belief that you are to blame for some unpleasant consequence, because you did something wrong. The feeling that you are responsible for another's hurt feelings.

Role: A part that one plays in the family. Each member of a dysfunctional family develops certain behaviors or characteristics to cope with unpredictable or invasive behavior of a parent. Each role—Hero, Mascot, Lost Child, or Scapegoat—fills a function in keeping the family together, and is very rigid and predictable. Roles lock each person into a set pattern of behavior.

Shame: The feeling that I am a mistake, that nothing you do will ever be good enough. Shame is similar to guilt, but shame does not relate to a specific incident or event, but rather to your entire life and self-worth.

Trash compactor: An imaginary storage tank for feelings that you want to avoid or deny. Whenever you feel painful feelings such as anger, sadness, or hurt, you push them into your trash compactor to hide them from yourself and/or others.

Taking Stock

TAKING STOCK

1 FAMILY ROLES (p 5)

Participants identify the characteristics of the role
(Enabler, Hero, Mascot, Lost Child, Scapegoat) they
played in their family of origin. (60–90 minutes)

2 FAMILY SCENES (p 11)

Participants recreate the dynamics of a dysfunctional
family by developing and presenting scenes with their
small group. (2–3 hours)

3 PERFECT FAMILY (p 16)

Participants discuss and write about the differences
between their perfect dream family and their imperfect
real family. (60 minutes)

4 BOUNDARIES (P 20)

In this brief exercise, participants determine their own
boundaries by experimenting with physical closeness.
(10 minutes)

5 SECRETS (P 22)

A powerful exercise in which participants anonymously
share personal secrets. (90 minutes)

6 WORK ADDICTION (P 25)

Participants use the **Work Addiction Risk Test** to look
at the role work plays in their lives, and then develop a
plan to moderate unhealthy work patterns.
(60–75 minutes)

TAKING STOCK

Work addiction, keeping harmful secrets, constantly attempting to solve the problems of others, avoiding anger—all sorts of problems have their roots in the past, especially for those who grew up in dysfunctional families. The exercises in this section help participants take stock of what happened to them when growing up, understand their behavior and work toward change.

Why look back? People who grew up in a dysfunctional family have a damaged sense of their own worth. They are told in many ways that they are no good. A parent may have hit them, made fun of them, corrected them constantly, forced too much responsibility on them, or overwhelmed them with guilt. In spite of that, people often have trouble seeing that their parents have hurt them. Facing, and then disconnecting from, traumas of the past helps people make positive changes.

In a dysfunctional family, people learn to ignore or invalidate their feelings and experiences. As they silence their inner voices, they become numb. When asked how they feel, they often do not know.

Without intervention, they may repeat the cycle. Since they are used to tip-toeing around a demanding parent, they often choose life partners who also are demanding, who have continual crises or problems. Just as in the original family, only one person's feelings and needs are important. The other person must continue to avoid and deny painful feelings, stuffing them into her internal trash compactor as if her feelings were garbage.

After years of this treatment, the garbage becomes unidentifiable and begins to stink. The person can no longer identify her feelings, but she knows something is wrong. This something can become translated into depression, anxiety, self-destructive behavior, or physical illness such as ulcers or colitis.

The exercises in this section will help participants empty out their trash compactors and examine their feelings openly, for the first time in a long time. Feelings are even scarier when they've been hidden and repressed for years, so people may be very resistant and fearful about participating in these exercises. Facilitators should be gently encouraging, while acknowledging that participants are responsible for their own behavior, growth, and pace.

Keep in mind that in the past, participants may have received very little respect for their needs. As a facilitator, you can respect them by letting them decide how involved they want to be. Remember, there is no perfection, just progress. Your job is simply to encourage them along the way.

©1994 Whole Person Press 210 W Michigan Duluth MN 55802   (800) 247-6789

1   FAMILY ROLES

Participants identify the characteristics of the role (Enabler, Hero, Mascot, Lost Child, Scapegoat) they played in their family of origin.

GOALS

Recognize the role or roles you played in a dysfunctional family system.

Identify the ways you play this role in your current family or relationships.

Identify the ways you play this role at work.

GROUP SIZE

Unlimited

TIME FRAME

60–90 minutes

MATERIALS NEEDED

Copies of the **Typical Dysfunctional Family Roles** handout and the **Family Roles** worksheet; newsprint, tape, and markers.

PROCESS

1) The facilitator gives an overview of the dysfunctional family system. (5–10 minutes)

- Those who grow up in a chaotic, painful, or unpredictable family setting learn to tip-toe around a parent who is abusive, alcoholic, rigid, invalidating, etc.

- Like a well-balanced mobile, each family member adjusts to the pivotal parent. Everyone reacts to this parent.

- This balancing allows the dysfunction to remain secret and unspoken. But each family member develops a role to play to cope with the emotional distress and tension.

- All of the coping roles are designed to relieve tension or provide some distraction from the dysfunctional situation.

- Each role helps the family put up a good front in a "crazy-making" environment. Yet these roles make it hard to be yourself and to have your own feelings. The cheerful family clown or mascot, for example, can't express anger.

- As you get older, unless you consciously work to change, you unconsciously continue to play this role. The dysfunction in the family of origin is then carried to the next generation. This is especially true when no intervention or recovery work is done.

2) The facilitator asks group members to write down a list of ways that they tip-toed around one or both parents. (5 minutes)

3) The facilitator distributes copies of the **Typical Dysfunctional Family Roles** handout.

4) The facilitator writes the name of each role on the blackboard or newsprint, discusses the characteristics of each role, and asks participants which role or roles they think they played.

5) The facilitator distributes the **Family Roles** worksheet and asks participants to fill it out. (10 minutes)

☞ *Some people may identify with more than one role, and may have shifted from one to another. This shift is sometimes due to a change in the family such as a death, a sibling leaving the household, or someone becoming mentally or physically ill. Ask those identifying with more than one role to write about the role they felt was most difficult, hurtful or uncomfortable.*

6) The facilitator gives the following instructions:

➤ Form groups of 5–7 people, according to the role you played (i.e., enablers in one group, heroes in another, etc.).

➤ I want you to discuss the questions on the worksheet, noting the strengths and weaknesses associated with each role.

➤ Choose one person from your group to record the group's responses on the newsprint.

7) After 20–30 minutes, the facilitator reconvenes the large group and asks the recorders from the small groups to tape their group's newsprint to the wall and to summarize the highlights of the group's discussion.

8) The facilitator asks the entire group these questions:

✔ What similar emotions and activities do you see in the different roles?

✔ What differences do you see between the different roles?

✔ How was stress handled by the people who played the roles?

9) The facilitator concludes the exercise by saying, "As you go about making changes, pick small behaviors to change, be consistent, and work patiently and slowly."

TRAINER'S NOTES

TYPICAL DYSFUNCTIONAL FAMILY ROLES

ENABLER/HELPER/LOVER

The enabler brings nurturance and a sense of belonging to the family. This job involves keeping everyone together, preserving the family unit at any cost (including physical violence or even death), and trying to smooth ruffled feathers. Often what motivates the enabler is the fear that other family members cannot stand on their own two feet. The enabler/helper/ lover may show seriousness, martyrdom, hypochondria, self-blame, self-pity, manipulation, and powerlessness, while inside she feels hurt, despair, anger, pain, self-doubt, guilt, fear, failure, fatigue, and self-doubt.

HERO

The hero provides self-esteem for the family and is often the oldest. She may go to medical school and become a famous surgeon, but secretly she feels awful because she has a sister in a mental hospital or a brother who has died of a cocaine overdose. Yet she carries the family banner for all the public to see. She makes the family proud, but pays a terrible price in terms of her own well-being. The hero may be quite successful, work hard for approval, be a perfectionist, put others first, appear special and "all together," be compulsive about achievement, and seem independent from the rest of the family. Inside the hero feels guilt, hurt, inadequacy, confusion, and frustration.

MASCOT

The mascot, who is often one of the younger children, provides humor and comic relief for the family. He gives the family a sense of fun, playfulness, silliness and a distorted type of joy. The cost to the mascot is that his true feelings of pain and isolation are never expressed. He remains emotionally underdeveloped until he begins a recovery program of his own. Outwardly, the mascot appears hyperactive, fragile, cute, wiry, tense, free-floating, manipulative, clowning, charming, immature. He displays attention-getting behavior and often has superficial social skills. On the inside, he may feel fear, guilt, anxiety, insecurity, confusion, loneliness or craziness.

SCAPEGOAT

The scapegoat usually acts out all the family's dysfunctions and, therefore, takes the blame and "the heat" for the family. He may be drug addicted or a thief. He is the "black sheep" who may get in fights or act out sexually. The family then gets to say, "If little brother weren't such a delinquent, our family would be fine." The cost to the scapegoat is obvious. He may be withdrawn, sullen, defiant, irresponsible, self-destructive, and rebellious. On the inside he is feeling hurt, anger, fear, shame, self-hate, rejection, and loneliness.

LOST CHILD/LONER

The lost child deals with the family dysfunction by escaping. In a sense, however, this family member is taking care of the family's needs for separateness and autonomy. This may be the child who stays in her room much of the time, or goes out in the woods to play by herself. She is alone, but it is not a healthy aloneness. A deep loneliness pervades those who play out this role. The lost child appears withdrawn, quiet, distant, intense, and independent. She rarely makes demands, and usually plays it safe. On the inside she may be lonely, hurt, sad, confused, fearful, and feeling worthless, pained and inadequate.

FAMILY ROLES

Role I most identify with   ❏ Enabler   ❏ Scapegoat
(Pick the role that was   ❏ Hero   ❏ Lost Child
the most central one to
you, the one that was   ❏ Mascot
most difficult or hurtful.)

Write out answers to these questions:

1. In what ways did you play out your role in your family of origin?	2. What feelings did you have to give up in this role?
3. What do you do now to play out this role in your current family or relationships?	4. How do you behave at work that is consistent with this role?
5. What changes would you like to make at home or work?	6. What other role do you want or like? Why?
7. What new behavior can you choose?	

2   FAMILY SCENES

Participants recreate the dynamics of a dysfunctional family by developing and presenting scenes with their small group.

GOALS

Recognize the role or roles you played in a dysfunctional family system.

Identify the roles you played in particularly stressful situations by acting out a scene.

GROUP SIZE

15 or more

TIME FRAME

2–3 hours

MATERIALS NEEDED

Copies of the **Typical Dysfunctional Family Roles** handout and the **Family Roles** worksheet (from the preceding exercise); newsprint, tape, and markers; TV, VCR, and videotape of a ½-hour situation comedy or segment of a film that shows a dysfunctional family.

> ☞ *Since this exercise takes 2–3 hours, it is best used in an all-day workshop or if participants have had an hour to plan in a previous session.*

PROCESS

1) The facilitator gives an overview of the dysfunctional family system. (5–10 minutes)

- Those who grow up in a chaotic, painful, or unpredictable family setting learn to tip-toe around a parent who is abusive, alcoholic, rigid, invalidating, etc.

- Like a well-balanced mobile, each family member adjusts to the pivotal parent. Everyone reacts to this parent.

- This balancing allows the dysfunction to remain secret and unspoken. But each family member develops a role to play to cope with the emotional distress and tension.

- All of the coping roles are designed to relieve tension or provide some distraction from the dysfunctional situation.

- Each role helps the family put up a good front in a "crazy-making" environment. Yet these roles make it hard to be yourself and to have your own feelings. The cheerful family clown or mascot, for example, can't express anger.

- As you get older, unless you consciously work to change, you unconsciously continue to play this role. The dysfunction in the family of origin is then carried to the next generation. This is especially true when no intervention or recovery work is done.

2) The facilitator asks group members to write down a list of ways that they tip-toed around one or both parents. (5 minutes)

3) The facilitator distributes copies of the **Typical Dysfunctional Family Roles** handout.

4) The facilitator writes the name of each role on the blackboard or newsprint, discusses the characteristics of each role, and asks participants which role or roles they think they played.

5) The facilitator shows the videotape to demonstrate the roles played in a dysfunctional family.

6) When the videotape ends, the facilitator asks the following questions:

✔ What roles did each person play?

✔ What were the characteristics of each role?

7) The facilitator distributes copies of the handout **Scene from a Dysfunctional Family**, then asks the participants to answer the following questions. As the group provides ideas, the facilitator writes them on the blackboard or newsprint.

✔ How could you demonstrate dysfunctional communication?

✔ What situations would show how family members play different roles?

✔ What are some examples of especially stressful times (e.g., Christmas dinner, the family talking with a school counselor about Johnny's attendance problem)?

8) The facilitator asks participants to form groups of 6–7 people and to select a scene to act out by taking ideas from the examples written on the blackboard or newsprint.

☞ *Some groups may pick the same scene. This is fine, as the scene will be developed differently by each group. The entire process may take up to an hour, but it is an important learning experience. Some participants may begin to look for props or wander around. Observe and take notes. You can later ask the group members to reflect on how they acted in the preparation process, the role they played in the scene itself, and how they acted in their families of origin. Ask if there are similarities. Make yourself available for questions.*

9) After each group has developed its scene, the facilitator asks participants to clear space in the middle of the room for the scenes to be presented.

10) The facilitator helps the groups decide the order in which the scenes will be presented.

☞ *Participants may get nervous as they wait. It is less stressful to know, rather than guess, when they will perform.*

11) One at a time, the facilitator asks the groups to present their 10-minute scenes.

12) After each scene, the facilitator asks questions to the audience and to the presenters.

To the audience:

✔ What did you notice about the interactions of the family members?

✔ Who did you identify with most, and why?

✔ What were the characteristics of each role (lost child, enabler, etc.)?

To the presenters:

✔ How did you feel playing this role?

✔ What behaviors made you angry?

✔ What made you laugh?

✔ How have you changed since childhood?

✔ As you prepared the scene, what did you notice about your style of participation? Was it similar to the role you played in the scene or similar to the role you played in your family of origin?

☞ *There may be sadness, joy, and other feelings felt and expressed. This is a good time to laugh with participants and to help them see*

---

the humor as well as the sadness in the restrictions of each role. Acting out their old roles may push people back into old behaviors. Encourage them to move out of the role they just played as they discuss the scene.

TRAINER'S NOTES

©1994 Whole Person Press 210 W Michigan Duluth MN 55802   (800) 247-6789

SCENE FROM A DYSFUNCTIONAL FAMILY

STRUCTURE

In groups of 6–8 people, work together to develop a scene that you will present to the others in the group. First the group decides on what the scene will be about, then each member chooses a family role to play. There may be characters with alcohol problems, anorexics or bulimics, compulsive achievers, withdrawn younger siblings, victims of incest, obsessive organizers, and distracting clowns. Each role should demonstrate some dysfunctional behavior.

The scenario should be about 10 minutes in length with enough time to show all the roles. Present a slice of life from the family. After you have developed the characters and the goals of the scene, practice to refine the scene so that it demonstrates the communication problems in the dysfunctional family.

PURPOSE

The purpose of this activity is to demonstrate the communication difficulties in a family with dysfunctional patterns. Denial and avoidance will provide a strong base, and each member may be involved in secrets, silence, withdrawal, and isolation. However, there may be a family member who has begun to recover or to become more healthy, in which case you can demonstrate how the rest of the family responds to this person (usually showing resistance to change), and how this person feels.

©1994 Whole Person Press 210 W Michigan Duluth MN 55802   (800) 247-6789

3   PERFECT FAMILY

Participants discuss and write about the differences between their perfect dream family and their imperfect real family.

GOALS

Identify the characteristics of a "perfect family."

List the oppressive rules that controlled interaction in participants real families.

GROUP SIZE

6–10 members

TIME FRAME

60 minutes

MATERIALS NEEDED

Props (optional), paper and pencils, copies of the **Family Rules Scale.**

PROCESS

1) The facilitator asks participants to write down characteristics of their ideal family by having them answer the following questions:

   ✔ In your perfect family, would you talk about your day with all the family members present?

   ✔ In your perfect family, if you were being pressured to drink alcohol, what would your parents say?

   ✔ In your perfect family, what might you do if you had a problem?

   ✔ In your perfect family, would your father start yelling if you told him you flunked a test? What would he do?

2) After 5–10 minutes, the facilitator distributes copies of the **Family Rules Scale** and asks participants to rate their family of origin. (10–15 minutes)

3) The facilitator writes the following questions on the blackboard or newsprint and asks participants to write answers to these questions:

✔ How did you feel as you rated your family?

✔ Who did the most criticizing in your family?

✔ What family rules do you still follow?

✔ What family rules are you breaking by answering the worksheet questions honestly?

4) After 10 minutes, the facilitator asks participants to call out any oppressive family rules that they experienced. She lists them on the blackboard or newsprint.

> ☞ *You may want to provide examples from your own life—saying, for example, "When I was sad, I was supposed to go to my room and think about all the other people in the world who had it worse than me." (The rule was "don't be selfish.") Or, "If I was mad, I was told it was impolite to say so, and I should keep it to myself." (The rule was "feelings, especially anger, should be kept to yourself and not expressed openly.")*

5) The facilitator lists the following rules if they are not brought up by the group:

- It is not okay to talk about problems.

- Communication should be indirect.

- Be strong, be good, be right, be perfect, make us proud.

- Do as I say, not as I do.

- It is not okay to play.

- You must always look good.

- Do not rock the boat.

6) The facilitator ends the discussion by making the following points:

- Rocking the boat is healthy in many situations. Being honest causes waves, and most of us have been trained to keep the peace at the expense of honesty. We deny our own feelings.

- We learn about the perfect family in every form of media: We see them on TV shows and in commercials; we read about them in novels.

- This media image of the perfect family clashes with what we experience in our own imperfect families and makes us feel ashamed.

©1994 Whole Person Press 210 W Michigan Duluth MN 55802   (800) 247-6789

- We want to hide the truth about our family.

- Hiding the truth creates problems for us.

7) The facilitator asks participants to circle the two rules from the **Family Rules Scale** that most damaged their self-esteem.

8) The facilitator asks participants to form groups of 4 and gives them the following instructions:

> ➤ Share with each other the two rules you picked and how you feel about them today.

> ➤ Discuss ways you'd like to change these two rules as you form new relationships.

9) The facilitator reconvenes the large group and asks participants for reactions.

☞ *Point out that these are common experiences and that talking with others is a way to ease the distress and anxiety.*

☞ *This exercise can be followed by the **Public vs. Private Self** exercise in the **Journaling** section.*

TRAINER'S NOTES

FAMILY RULES SCALE

Mark where you think your family was on the scale.

1. My family talked about problems.

Seldom   Sometimes   Frequently

_____

2. Feelings were expressed openly in my family.

Seldom   Sometimes   Frequently

_____

3. Communication was direct in my family.

Seldom   Sometimes   Frequently

_____

4. Mistakes were accepted without great criticism in my family.

Seldom   Sometimes   Frequently

_____

5. It was okay to do things just for yourself in my family.

Seldom   Sometimes   Frequently

_____

6. Playing and fun was encouraged in my family.

Seldom   Sometimes   Frequently

_____

7. My family thought it was okay to look messy in public.

Seldom   Sometimes   Frequently

_____

8. It was okay to rock the boat by disagreeing with my parents.

Seldom   Sometimes   Frequently

_____

4   BOUNDARIES

In this brief exercise, participants determine their own boundaries by experimenting with physical closeness.

GOALS

Identify individual physical boundaries.

Examine factors that affect where boundaries are set.

GROUP SIZE

Unlimited

TIME FRAME

10–20 minutes

MATERIALS NEEDED

None

PROCESS

1) The facilitator gives the following instructions:

   ➤ Stand and choose a partner whom you do not know well.

   ➤ One person in each pair should stand still while the other person moves 8–10 feet away.

   ➤ The person standing still tells the other person to begin walking towards him.

   ➤ He tells the person to stop when he first feels uncomfortable with the closeness.

2) After everyone does this once, the facilitator tells participants to change roles and repeat the process.

3) As participants remain standing, the facilitator asks these questions:

   ✔ At what distance did you recognize your boundary?

   ✔ Were you surprised by your boundary?

   ✔ When you were the one moving, were you allowed to get closer than was comfortable for you? How did that feel?

   ✔ Do you feel more comfortable being close to someone of the same or opposite sex?

   ✔ Who are the people you allow to be close to you?

   ✔ What are the differences in your boundaries at work and at home?

   ✔ Are your physical boundaries and emotional boundaries similar?

4) The facilitator gives the following instructions:

   ➤ Choose another person (again someone you do not know well).

   ➤ Repeat the walking and stopping exercise, intentionally altering your boundaries (enlarging or contracting).

5) As the participants finish, the facilitator asks what was different for them this time, and why.

6) The facilitator tells the group to sit down and leads a discussion by asking the following questions:

   ✔ What insights do you have about boundaries and limits?

   ✔ How do comfort zones in various cultures differ? (For example, in Hispanic cultures, the comfort zone is often closer than in the white North American culture.)

   ✔ What differences in comfort zones occurred with same-sex partners versus opposite-sex partners? (Men often learn that touch and close contact is related primarily to sexuality, while women often associate touch with affection, rather than just sex.)

   ✔ Boundaries are based on experiences, culturally learned rules, gender differences, and familiarity with the other person. Are there other factors that affect your boundaries?

   ☞ *This exercise can lead to discussions about how participants' physical and emotional space was invaded by parents who did not respect their needs for privacy or self determination. A mother may have read a child's diary. A father may have tickled a child without regard for his comfort. Boundaries are affected by these invasive experiences. The exercise A **Child's Needs** (later in this section) addresses these concerns.*

5 SECRETS

A powerful exercise in which participants anonymously share personal secrets.

GOALS

Identify and share a personal secret that has never been revealed to others.

Experience empathy from others who hear about or *own* the secret.

GROUP SIZE

6 or more

TIME FRAME

90 minutes

MATERIALS NEEDED

Paper and pencils; at least one hat for each group; blackboard or newsprint.

PROCESS

1) The facilitator introduces the exercise with the following points:

- Dysfunctional families have some basic rules of avoidance and denial of feelings and of events. As a result, secrets develop. These secrets create a sense of confusion, self-doubt, and blame, especially for children. This leads to frozen feelings or numbness.

- Secrets make people feel lonely, different, isolated, and frightened.

- Secrets allow people to hide and to be dishonest with themselves and others. Interpersonal relationships are limited and emotional intimacy is avoided.

- Sharing secrets and receiving understanding responses helps break the spell of isolation. People can begin to feel closer and experience emotional intimacy.

2) The facilitator asks participants to form groups of 6–8 people, with friends and work groups being separate, and gives each group a hat.

3) The facilitator hands out a blank piece of paper to each participant (each sheet should be the same size and color) and gives the following instructions:

➤ Write down a secret that you have never shared before. Make sure you have privacy as you write.

➤ You will not be reading your own secret to anyone. This exercise is anonymous.

➤ Do not use any names or identifiers.

➤ If you really don't want to write down a secret, you can choose not to. This is your choice, but please turn in a blank piece of paper so that no one can identify you.

4) After 3 minutes, the facilitator has participants fold their secrets and put them in the hat belonging to their group. She then gives the following instructions:

➤ One at a time, please take a secret out of the hat. Do this slowly, drawing one secret at a time.

➤ If you draw your own secret, return it and choose another one.

➤ Now one at a time, you will read the secret you have picked and describe to the group what you believe it would be like to live with that secret.

☞ *It is important to observe the groups, and to be aware if individuals become upset. Be available to talk to individuals and groups and to intervene if you see that someone needs support.*

5) After all the secrets and descriptions of feelings are shared, ask participants to return to the large group. The facilitator writes the following questions on the blackboard or newsprint, and asks participants to write their responses to these questions:

✔ What was your reaction when the exercise was first described?

✔ What is your reaction now that it is over and you have heard your secret read aloud and responded to by others in the group?

✔ What was it like to read another person's secret and react to it?

6) After 10 minutes, ask participants to share their responses. Ask one question at a time.

☞ *This exercise can make people feel very vulnerable. People may admit that they are gay or lesbian, or may reveal that they were sexually abused. Be ready to accept the secrets, and allow time to talk with people individually after the exercise. You may need to refer people to other resources for help and support. Allow time afterwards for people to talk with each other and mingle, so they can continue to offer each other support.*

TRAINER'S NOTES

6   WORK ADDICTION

Participants use the **Work Addiction Risk Test** to look at the role work plays in their lives, and then develop a plan to moderate unhealthy work patterns.

GOALS

Assess the degree of work addiction.

Identify your specific risk areas for work-addiction behavior.

Create a plan to modify work addiction behaviors.

GROUP SIZE

5 or more

TIME FRAME

60–75 minutes

MATERIALS NEEDED

Copies of **Work Addiction Risk Test (WART)**, **Steven's Work Moderation Plan**, and **My Work Moderation Plan.**

PROCESS

1) The facilitator introduces the exercise by outlining the following concepts:

- In dysfunctional families, where the goal is to avoid and deny painful feelings, some people choose to overeat or take drugs. Others choose to "over-do."

- When they are successful, work addicts get the positive reinforcement (money, prestige, respect) that they did not get as children. But they may very well be using work to avoid interacting with family, thinking about the death of a parent, or feeling the pain from childhood sexual abuse.

- Work addiction is not like drug addiction. It is good to work, but you need to stop using work to avoid difficult feelings and interactions.

---

2) The facilitator asks participants to complete the **WART** (**Work Addiction Risk Test**) and add up their total score. (10 minutes)

3) The facilitator asks participants to circle the numbers of three items from the **WART** that they believe are especially important issues for them.

4) The facilitator distributes **Steven's Work Moderation Plan** and **My Work Moderation Plan** and goes over the **Steven's Plan**, making the following points:

> ➤ You will develop a plan for altering your work addiction behavior, using as your target one of the three behaviors you circled on the **WART**.

> ➤ The first step is to define the behavior. You can see on **Steven's Plan** how specific you need to be. In the example, working late was the behavior targeted for change.

> ➤ The second step is to think of concrete ways that you could change that behavior. In Steven's plan, he is going to try to leave with his colleagues three times a week instead of staying late every night.

> ➤ In the third step, you outline how you will keep track of the behavior you are trying to change. In Steven's plan, he is going to keep an actual written record.

> ➤ The fourth step is to look ahead to how it is going to feel to change this behavior. It may seem like a small change, but it may make you very anxious. In Steven's plan, he anticipates feeling anxious and scared about the family reaction.

> ➤ Now fill out **My Work Moderation Plan**. Customize your plan to your own issues, schedules, work situation, and rewards.

> ➤ You have 10 minutes.

5) The facilitator asks participants to break into small groups of 4–6 people according to the small group name that they think best fits them. The groups are: *Hard workers, Over achievers, Slouches, Compulsive procrastinators, Perfectionists.*

> ☞ *If only one person picks a particular group, ask her to make a second choice. If no one picks a certain group, that is fine. There may be lots of hard workers and no slouches. Be sure there are only 4–6 people in each group, even if it means dividing a group.*

6) Once people are in small groups, the facilitator asks them to discuss their plans to change work behaviors, considering the following questions:

✔ Is the plan practical?

✔ Will the plan work?

✔ Is it specific enough?

✔ Do you think you will be better off if you implement the plan?

> ☞ *Participants may need a lot of encouragement to stay on task, although the true work addict will go right at the job and try to complete it perfectly! Make sure that each person ends the exercise with a written plan.*

> ☞ *My Loves, Befriending Your Child, and Play Group exercises in the Healing Patterns section show participants how to gradually moderate work addiction by having them act silly and childlike.*

TRAINER'S NOTES

STEVEN'S WORK MODERATION PLAN

1. Pick one item from WART that you want to moderate.

   Item 15, "I find myself continuing to work after my co-workers have called it quits."

2. How can I recognize work-addictive behavior as it happens?

   I will keep a log for two weeks noting the usual time that most of my peers leave work, and noting the time when I leave work.

3. What changes can I make in daily routines to modify work-addictive behavior?

   Once I have this information in writing, I may decide that three days each week I will leave work when others usually leave, regardless of the work I must leave behind.

4. What method will I use to keep track of the changes that I am making?

   I could keep a log of the times I leave the office and of the feelings I have when I leave with others.

5. What feelings do I anticipate as I make these changes?

   I expect that I will be anxious and scared as I leave work behind and face some things that I have ignored in my life. I am afraid I will not be accepted by my family as I try to spend more time with them.

6. What will I do to reward myself for modifying my work-addictive behavior?

   Once I leave early 10 times, I will invite a friend out to dinner to celebrate.

©1994 Whole Person Press 210 W Michigan Duluth MN 55802   (800) 247-6789

MY WORK MODERATION PLAN

1. Pick one item from WART that you want to moderate.

2. How can I recognize work-addictive behavior as it happens?

3. What changes can I make in daily routines to modify work-addictive behavior?

4. What method will I use to keep track of the changes that I am making?

5. What feelings do I anticipate as I make these changes?

6. What will I do to reward myself for modifying my work-addictive behavior?

WORK ADDICTION RISK TEST (WART)

Read each of the twenty-five statements below and decide how much each one pertains to you. Use this rating scale:

1-never true; 2-seldom true; 3-often true; 4-always true

Enter the number that best fits your behavior.

_____	1. I prefer to do most things myself rather than ask for help.
_____	2. I get very impatient when I have to wait for someone or something.
_____	3. I seem to be in a hurry, racing against the clock.
_____	4. I get irritated when I am interrupted.
_____	5. I stay busy and keep many "irons in the fire."
_____	6. I find myself doing two or three things at one time, such as eating lunch and writing a memo while talking on the telephone.
_____	7. I overly commit myself by biting off more than I can chew.
_____	8. I feel guilty when I am not working on something.
_____	9. It is important that I see the concrete results of what I do.
_____	10. I am more interested in the final result of my work than in the process.
_____	11. Things just never seem to get done fast enough for me.
_____	12. I lose my temper when things don't go my way or work out to suit me.
_____	13. I ask the same question over again, without realizing it, after I've already been given the answer once.
_____	14. I spend a lot of time planning and thinking about future events while tuning out the here and now.
_____	15. I find myself continuing to work after my co-workers have quit.
_____	16. I get angry when people don't meet my standards of perfection.
_____	17. I get upset when I am in situations I cannot control.
_____	18. I tend to put myself under pressure with self-imposed deadlines.
_____	19. It is hard for me to relax when I'm not working.
_____	20. I spend more time working than I do on hobbies, leisure activities, or socializing with friends.
_____	21. I dive into projects to get a head start before all the phases have been finalized.
_____	22. I get upset with myself for making even the smallest mistake.
_____	23. I put more thought, time, and energy into my work than I do into my relationships with my spouse (or lover) and family.
_____	24. I forget, ignore, or minimize important family celebrations such as birthdays, reunions, anniversaries, or holidays.
_____	25. I make important decisions before I have all the facts or have a chance to think them through.

A score of 25 to 54 indicates you are not work addicted; 55 to 69 mildly work addicted; 70 to 100 highly work addicted.

Reprinted with the permission of the publishers, Health Communications, Inc., Deerfield Beach, FL, from Work Addiction *by Bryan E. Robinson, Ph.D. © 1989.*

7   ANGER: WHO AND HOW

Participants assess how they experience and express anger. They explore how anger was handled in their family of origin, as well as its role in their current relationship.

GOALS

Identify how anger was and is expressed in the family of origin.

Identify how anger is felt and expressed now.

Identify how anger can control an individual's behavior.

GROUP SIZE

6 or more

TIME FRAME

90 minutes

MATERIALS NEEDED

Paper, pencil and crayons; blackboard or newsprint.

PROCESS

1) The facilitator asks participants to list 5 ways that people in their current living situation express anger. (5 minutes)

2) The facilitator asks participants to form groups of 6–8 people.

3) The facilitator asks participants to discuss their list with other group members. The facilitator writes the following questions, one at a time, on the blackboard or newsprint as a guide for the discussion.

> ☞ *Let participants discuss each question for 5 minutes before you write the next one.*

✔ Do men and women express anger differently?

✔ Where do the other people in your living situation go when they are angry? What do they do?

✔ Where do you go when you are angry? What do you do?

✔ When someone shows anger, how do you react?

4) After 20 minutes, while participants are still sitting in groups, the facilitator asks them to write down how people in their families of origin (mother, father, and any siblings) dealt with anger when they lived together. (5 minutes)

> ☞ *This assignment allows participants to see how people in their current living situation deal with anger (addressed in step 1) compared with how people in their family of origin dealt with anger. Often a current relationship difficulty mirrors a situation with a difficult family member. The facilitator asks people to compare the two and make some observations.*

5) After 5 minutes the facilitator asks participants to stay in small groups and to share what they wrote about anger in their families of origin.

6) Reconvene the large group and ask participants for insights about anger and the expression of it in their families of origin, making sure that the following points are raised:

- Anger is a feeling. Violence is an action. When people live in families where anger was expressed as violence, anger may be particularly scary.

- Some people avoid expressing anger altogether because they are afraid of losing control—of "blowing up."

- Some people seem to exude anger and defensiveness regularly (they are stiff and glaring), and still claim they are not mad.

- Some people hold anger inside and get physically ill (i.e. ulcer, colitis). Many people find it difficult to express anger in appropriate ways.

- People differ in their ability to express anger directly, honestly and without violence.

7) The facilitator asks participants to make a crayon drawing of their own anger. (5 minutes)

> ☞ *Encourage people to be creative. Tell them to just scribble and draw as they choose, as quickly and freely as they can, without thinking too much. Just draw!*

8) The facilitator asks participants to go back to their small groups. The facilitator writes the following questions on the board as a guide for the small group discussion.

✔ What does your anger look like?

✔ Who sees your anger and what do they see?

✔ What color is it?

✔ How do you feel about it?

✔ What colors did you use in your drawing?

✔ How thick were the lines?

✔ Where was your drawing placed on the page?

✔ How do differences in these elements make you feel about the drawing?

9) After 20 minutes, the facilitator gathers the large group together and asks participants for observations and insights about what they learned, making the following points if they do not come up in the discussion.

- A person may deny being angry while withdrawing and not talking to anyone. He may slam the door and make the car tires squeal as he drives away.

- Someone may bring up something she is angry about days, weeks, or years later. Often it happens in a fight.

- Men often learn aggressive ways of expressing anger, such as slamming doors, hitting, withdrawing emotionally, or leaving the house. Women are more likely to cry or do something passive-aggressive such as act cheery and then burn dinner. Women isolate themselves in the house and often go to the bedroom.

  ☞ *It is possible that through this exercise some people will uncover anger that they didn't know about. Often people will say, "I thought I was over that," or "I didn't realize that I was still mad at my father about this." Be ready to take a break, talk with individuals further, or refer them to a professional to help them deal with their anger.*

  ☞ *For more extended work on anger, refer to the **Assertiveness** exercise in the **Healing Patterns** section.*

©1994 Whole Person Press 210 W Michigan Duluth MN 55802   (800) 247-6789

8   RIPPLES

In this exercise participants move cherished objects of the group's members as a way to reveal group dynamics and individual needs.

GOALS

Demonstrate the relationship dynamics in an established group.

Reduce tension between members of the group.

GROUP SIZE

6–10

TIME FRAME

30 minutes

MATERIALS NEEDED

Table and participants' valued objects.

> ☞ *Prior to the session in which you use this exercise, tell participants to bring in a valued object, such as a special rock, tie, plant, pen, or book, that reflects something about who they are.*

PROCESS

This exercise is appropriate for work groups, families, support or therapy groups that have met several times, committees that have worked together for some time, or church groups whose members know each other. This exercise provides a forum to help members see how sub-groups develop, to see who wants control and who withdraws from participation.

1) The facilitator gives the following instructions:

➤ Please remain silent throughout the first part of the exercise.

➤ Place your valued object on the empty table, in any position you wish.

➤ Now stand in a circle around the table.

➤ One at a time, please move any single object, except for your own, to a different position on the table. Do this slowly, and pause 5 seconds between each move.

☞ *Some people will remain uninvolved and may mostly watch others move objects, while others will be very active, moving many objects. This process can be revealing of patterns in the group.*

2) The facilitator allows this process to continue for 5 minutes, or until each person has had three or four turns at moving an object, or until most people stop moving things.

☞ *Remind participants that this is a silent exercise.*

3) While participants continue to stand around the table, the facilitator begins a discussion about the process, asking the following questions:

✔ What did you notice about the change in the position of the object that you brought?

✔ What objects were moved away from or toward other objects?

✔ Does the way certain objects were moved reflect the way you see relationships among people in this group?

✔ Who participated least? Who participated most?

✔ Do you notice any expression of anger, sadness, or other feelings in yourself or in others?

✔ How was your level of participation similar to how you usually function within this group?

☞ *Allow the discussion to go on for 20 minutes or until there is a natural pause.*

4) If there is a leader in the group (director, teacher) and especially a controlling one, the facilitator may ask the leader to leave the room during part of the discussion. For example, the facilitator may say, "Let's see what changes when the leader is absent."

☞ *The level of honesty and openness may increase in the absence of the leader. The leader may find this very difficult and frightening, and may fear having the group out of her control.*

5) The facilitator then asks participants the following questions:

✔ Was your behavior consistent with your behavior in other settings?

✔ How did you feel about your behavior during this exercise?

✔ What were your feelings at the time of the exercise and what are they now?

✔ When did you feel these feelings as a child?

☞ *Participants will often play a part in this exercise similar to the part they play in this group (and often other groups they belong to, such as families, social groups, etc.).*

6) The facilitator makes the following points to help participants discuss how they reacted to stress or pressure when they were children in a dysfunctional family, and how these same feelings come to light in their adult lives.

- Often you feel out of control, helpless, scared, and sometimes immobilized when you "feel little" (young) again.

- If your family was dysfunctional, and family members weren't allowed to express their feelings without fear, you can continue to experience feelings of numbness or helplessness as an adult.

- You may withdraw from relationships that require honesty and "presentness," as in this exercise. You might have stopped participating or tried to control the movement of the objects by participating a lot.

TRAINER'S NOTES

This exercise was developed by Gerry Howe, Morning Star Associates, West Branch, IA, author of Listen to the Heart: The Transformational Path to Health and Wellness, *Rudi Publishing, ©1991.*

9   RESCUING AND SOLVING

Through written work and discussions, participants learn about rescuing and explore ways to avoid the rescue triangle.

GOALS

Illustrate the patterns of rescuing and the rescue triangle.

Identify personal rescuing behaviors.

List personal rescuing behaviors that need to be changed.

GROUP SIZE

Unlimited

TIME FRAME

30 minutes

MATERIALS NEEDED

Copies of the **Rescuer's Checklist** and **Rhonda the Rescuer** handouts for each participant; blackboard or newsprint.

PROCESS

1) The facilitator asks participants to complete the **Rescuer's Checklist**. (10 minutes)

2) The facilitator leads a discussion, asking the following questions:

    ✔ What did you learn about yourself as you completed the checklist?

    ✔ How are you different at work and at home?

    ✔ Who in your family of origin acts in a similar way?

3) On the blackboard or newsprint, the facilitator draws the rescue triangle to illustrate the problems in rescuing others.

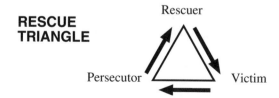

RESCUE TRIANGLE

4) Present the following points:

- Helping others feels good to most people. But when it is the primary method you use to help yourself feel good, it can get in the way of caring for yourself. People from dysfunctional families often satisfy their personal needs by helping, or trying to solve other people's problems.

- The band-aid or fix-it syndrome is easy to recognize. When a friend tells you about a problem, you listen and then say, "Why don't you do . . ." or "What if you tried . . ." You cannot stand for her to be in distress.

- You think that to be worth your salt, you must offer a solution that will make things all better. You want to rescue her from the dilemma.

- If she does not take your suggestion, or says she doesn't want advice, you think she doesn't like you.

- Helpers and solvers define their worth by how much they are able to "fix it" for others. When your offer of help is rejected, it is a personal injury. You feel like a victim and may think, *All I try to do is help, and all I get is people being mean to me.* This behavior is often part of the rescue triangle.

- When engaged in the rescue triangle you switch from rescuer, to victim, to persecutor, depending on the situation.

5) The facilitator distributes the **Rhonda the Rescuer** handout and reads it aloud to the group. Participants brainstorm ideas for how Rhonda can avoid getting caught up in the rescue triangle. Responses are written on the board.

6) The facilitator asks participants to look again at their completed **Rescuer's Checklist** and gives the following instructions:

➤ Pick 2 items from the checklist that you would work on to change.

➤ Pick 2 items that you would like to have stay the same.

➤ Now write the 2 items you want to change on 4 separate pieces of paper.

➤ When you get home or go back to work, post the items in a prominent place (refrigerator, mirror, in front of your desk).

➤ Record the number of times you do each of these things.

7) The facilitator should complete the exercise with these comments:

- Remember to think small and go slow regarding change. It is important to choose only 2 items to work on.

- Keep it simple and give yourself credit for small victories.

- Remember, the goal is to pay attention to what you do, so that you learn how you feel and act. Look inside for the feelings.

VARIATIONS

- The facilitator tells a personal story of getting caught in a rescue triangle, describing how each of the three roles in the rescue triangle were acted out. This is a good way to demonstrate how common such situations are.

- The facilitator asks participants to tell or write their own story about a time when they were caught in the rescue triangle. Tell them that it's okay to exaggerate or sound ridiculous—the point is to show how ludicrous the rescue trap really is.

TRAINER'S NOTES

RHONDA THE RESCUER

Rhonda worked in an agency that provided food service for a hotel. She was bright, funny, and a hard worker. She was well liked and had a lot of innovative ideas for improving the agency. Whenever other women in her work group complained about a problem, she was the first to offer a suggestion for change, and to try to "take care of" the problem. It was important to her to please other people, and she would do this by trying to fix things for others.

One day a co-worker, Paula, came to Rhonda and said, "I just don't know how I am going to get all the vendor orders completed in time to pick up my daughter from day care today." Rhonda said, "No problem, I will help you until you get them done." Paula was delighted, and Rhonda started working on the orders to rescue Paula. While Paula spent much of the rest of the day complaining to others about how much work she had to get done, Rhonda continued to work on Paula's orders. When 5:00 p.m. rolled around, Rhonda was still working on the orders and Paula quickly left, without a "thank you" or an acknowledgment of Rhonda's help. Rhonda was steaming mad as she was left there with the orders still incomplete. While Rhonda started out as a rescuer, she now felt like a victim. She felt that she was not appreciated, and had been used by Paula.

The rescue triangle was complete the next day when Rhonda started complaining to others about how lazy and unorganized Paula is at work. Rhonda had now become the persecutor. She expressed her anger and resentment by criticizing Paula, who could not get her own work done and did not appreciate Rhonda's help enough to thank her properly. Rhonda, in her efforts to jump in to save Paula from her own responsibilities, participated in the grand trio: the rescue-victim-persecutor triangle.

RESCUER'S CHECKLIST

Completing the checklist can help you become aware of ways you may be rescuing people without realizing it. It is taken, with permission, from the "Transactional Checklist."

Mark each of the statements below as it applies to you according to this code: 0 = seldom or never; 1 = sometimes or occasionally; and 2 = frequently. X = significant others in your life, such as spouse, boss, parents, friend, or colleague.

_____ 1. Is it hard for you to take time for yourself and have fun?

_____ 2. Do you supply words for X when s/he hesitates?

_____ 3. Do you set limits for yourself that you then exceed?

_____ 4. Do you believe you are responsible for making X happy?

_____ 5. Do you enjoy lending a shoulder for X to "cry" on?

_____ 6. Do you believe that X is not sufficiently grateful for your help?

_____ 7. Do you take care of X more than you take care of yourself?

_____ 8. Do you find yourself interrupting when X is talking?

_____ 9. Do you watch for clues for ways to be helpful to X?

_____ 10. Do you make excuses, openly or mentally, for X?

_____ 11. Do you do more than your share, that is, work harder than X?

_____ 12. When X is unsure or uncomfortable about doing something, do you do it for X?

_____ 13. Do you give up doing things because X wouldn't like it?

_____ 14. Do you believe that you really know what is best for X?

_____ 15. Do you think X would have grave difficulty getting along without you?

_____ 16. Do you use the word "we" and then find you don't have X's consent?

_____ 17. Do you stop yourself by thinking X will feel badly if you say or do something?

_____ 18. Is it hard for you not to respond to anyone who seems hurting or needing help?

_____ 19. Are you resented when you were only trying to be helpful?

_____ 20. Do you give advice that is not welcome or accepted?

_____ Total score. More than 10 points, rescuing is possible; more than 20 points, rescuing is probable.

From The Wellness Workbook *©1981, 1988 by John Travis and Regina Sara Ryan, published by Ten Speed Press, Berkely, CA.*

10 A CHILD'S NEEDS

In this simple, yet powerful, exercise, participants use crayons and their non-dominant hand to explore their own needs.

GOALS

Recall and identify feelings of need from childhood.

Experience childhood needs in a new way.

GROUP SIZE

6 or more

TIME FRAME

45–60 minutes

MATERIALS NEEDED

Paper and crayons; newsprint or blackboard.

PROCESS

1) The facilitator writes the following on the newsprint or blackboard: "As a child I need . . ."

2) She hands out crayons and blank paper and tells the participants to make a list of words or phrases to complete the phrase. (3–5 minutes)

   ☞ *Participants will naturally use their dominant hand to do this. Having them change hands later, with little warning, increases the power of the exercise.*

3) The facilitator asks participants to form groups of 6–8 people and writes the following questions on the board or newsprint for group discussion:

   ✔ What feelings did I have while writing my responses?

   ✔ What are my three most important needs?

   ✔ What are the similarities with other group members?

4) After 15–20 minutes, while participants remain in small groups, the facilitator gives the following instructions:

➤ Now use your non-dominant hand to make a list of words or phrases to complete the same sentence: "As a child I need . . . "

➤ If you have trouble doing this, take five deep breaths. It can also help to close your eyes and start writing.

☞ *Participants will often giggle, say they can't do this, and look around to see how others are doing. To encourage participants, do this exercise yourself on the blackboard or newsprint so others can see. Participants will begin to let go of some of their inhibitions.*

5) After 3–5 minutes, the facilitator makes a few points about the experience:

- Your child's view gets lost very early in life.

- When you grow up in dysfunctional families, you often are expected to function as an adult before you are ready.

- If you were a *really good kid*, chances are that many of your needs were ignored, buried, or unmet.

- Most adults learn to control their thoughts and to be rational. This is generally left-brain activity.

- When you use your dominant hand (the one you write with), your brain controls you and you may be less able to experience your feelings.

- When you use your non-dominant hand to write, you may be less controlled, more intuitive, more feeling, and more in touch with the childlike parts of yourself.

- This exercise allows your heart-felt feelings to emerge and lets you experience the difference between these two parts of you.

6) The facilitator writes the following questions on the blackboard or newsprint and asks participants to stay in the same small groups to discuss them:

✔ What feelings did I have while writing my responses?

✔ What was different this time with the other hand?

✔ What are the three most important needs that I had?

✔ What are the similarities with group members?

©1994 Whole Person Press 210 W Michigan Duluth MN 55802   (800) 247-6789

7) After 15–20 minutes, the facilitator reconvenes the large group, asks participants for feedback and comments, and makes these final points:

- You are generally encouraged as adults to hide, deny, and avoid childlike responses from yourself and others.

- This exercise is designed to use the right side of the brain, the creative, emotional, intuitive part, to explore your unacknowledged or unexplored needs and feelings.

TRAINER'S NOTES

11 SELF-ESTEEM

In this exercise participants recall experiences of childhood guilt and shame and consider how these feelings have affected their adult behavior.

GOALS

Identify specific experiences of guilt and shame from childhood.

Recognize how personal self-esteem affects current relationships.

GROUP SIZE

6 or more

TIME FRAME

60 minutes

MATERIALS NEEDED

Overhead transparency or large drawing of the **Model of Dysfunctional Patterns** and copies of the **Self-Esteem Worksheet.**

PROCESS

1) The facilitator shows the overhead or drawing of the **Model of Dysfunctional Patterns** and introduces the exercise by making the following points:

   - Guilt comes from the feeling that "I made a mistake," and shame comes from the feeling that "I am a mistake."

   - The **Model of Dysfunctional Patterns** shows the connection between addictive behaviors, which are the tip of the iceberg, and the identity and intimacy problems, hidden guilt, shame, and fear of abandonment that cause them.

   - When you are raised in a dysfunctional family, you are often ignored, yelled at, or told, in some fashion, not to express yourself.

   - You are likely to develop some of the addictive patterns shown in the model.

2) The facilitator distributes copies of the **Self-Esteem Worksheet** and asks participants to write answers to the questions in the top box.

3) The facilitator asks participants to form groups of 3–5 people to discuss their lists with one another. Moving from group to group, she encourages discussion by using the following questions along with examples from her own life.

✔ What is hard about sharing these lists?

✔ In what ways are your lists similar?

✔ What are the common denominators in these experiences?

4) While participants remain in their small groups, the facilitator asks them to take 5 minutes to fill in the bottom box of the worksheet. When most people are done, she goes to the next step.

5) The facilitator asks participants to discuss the following questions with the other group members:

✔ What is the connection between childhood guilt and shame and the way you feel about yourself now?

✔ What current actions are driven by the feeling that you can never be or do enough to feel okay about yourself?

6) After 15–20 minutes, the facilitator reconvenes the large group and reports their reactions to the exercise. She leads with the following question: "What did you learn about yourself and your similarity to others?"

Secrets, in this section, is a good follow-up exercise.

TRAINER'S NOTES

SELF-ESTEEM WORKSHEET

List times when, as a child, you felt guilty.

List times when, as a child, you felt ashamed.

List times when you felt like you could never be good enough at anything to please one of your parents.

List three things that you now do primarily to please another person.

List three people toward whom you currently show undeserved loyalty.

List three things that you do to compensate for low self-esteem.

MODEL OF DYSFUNCTIONAL PATTERNS

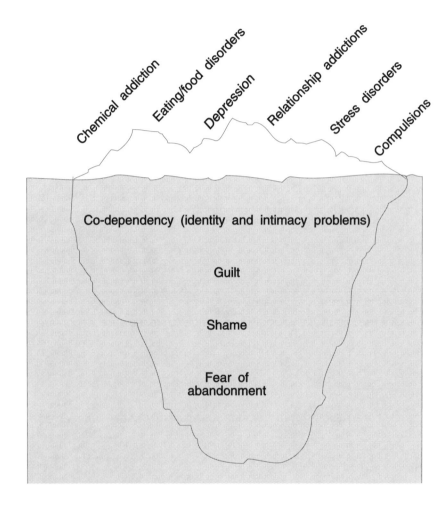

Reprinted with the permission of the publishers, Health Communications, Inc., Deerfield Beach, FL, from Adult Children: The Secrets of Dysfunctional Families *by John and Linda Friel, ©1988.*

12 RELATIONSHIP CHOICE

Participants compare the characteristics of their significant others to the characteristics they value most in a relationship.

GOALS

Identify and discuss characteristics of *ideal* relationships.

Compare ideal relationships with existing personal relationships.

Explain decisions that lead to relationships that are at odds with stated ideals.

GROUP SIZE

Unlimited

TIME FRAME

30 minutes

MATERIALS NEEDED

Copies of **Relationship Choice**; paper and pencils; blackboard; or newsprint.

PROCESS

1) The facilitator distributes the **Relationship Choice** worksheet and asks participants to complete it. (10 minutes)

2) The facilitator leads a discussion asking the following questions:

   ✔ What did it feel like to make each list?

   ✔ When you remembered a person who had the characteristics on List A, how did you feel?

   ✔ How do you feel about those relationships with the List A people?

3) The facilitator asks each participant to say which characteristic they have identified as the most important one. He then makes a list of these characteristics on the blackboard or newsprint.

4) The facilitator asks participants, "How did it feel to cross off ideal characteristics from the B list?"

5) The facilitator concludes the exercise by making the following points:

- It is not unusual for people to choose significant others who have characteristics similar to the ones dealt with in the family of origin.

  ☞ *Show relevant examples of this in your own life.*

- You may seek a relationship that meets needs that weren't met in childhood (e.g., trust and respect). These characteristics usually emerge in the group B list.

- There is often a big gap between the people you actually choose and what you believe is most important in a relationship. Do you have this kind of gap?

  ☞ *Some may say and/or believe that they do not deserve to be treated with respect and love. This low self-esteem causes pain and continued addictive behavior. Encourage them to seek counseling and offer information about local resources.*

TRAINER'S NOTES

RELATIONSHIP CHOICE

A. List 3 or 4 people (other than your family of origin) with whom you have had an important or significant relationship during the past five years.
1.   3.
2.   4.

B. Make a list of characteristics of the people in the list above. Examples include: affectionate, critical.
1.   6.
2.   7.
3.   8.
4.   9.
5.   10.

C. List the characteristics you would most want to find in people with whom you have a significant relationship.
1.   6.
2.   7.
3.   8.
4.   9.
5.   10.

D. Look at List A, and write below the names of any significant people from your childhood who had the characteristics on List B.
1.   3.
2.   4.

E. Return to List B and cross off all the characteristics but the five most important to you. Write those five here.
1 .   4.
2.   5.
3.

Cross off all but the three most important characteristics on the list above.

Cross off all but the one most important characteristic on the list above.

Write the most important characteristic here:

TRAINER'S NOTES

Journaling

JOURNALING

JOURNALING

Keeping a private journal is an important way to explore feelings, actions, and thoughts. But people from dysfunctional families often have difficulties acknowledging their feelings in any way. They may need the structure provided by a group to help them get started on the journaling process.

The nine exercises in this section use creative encouragements to help participants unlock their resistance to exploring their feelings. As participants "journal" their way through this section, they find a safe way to explore feelings of shame, obsession, guilt, and grief; and the difference between the image they present to the public and their "real," private selves.

For groups that meet several times, homework assignments such as journal writing extend and expand the process of self-exploration to life outside the group. People who come from dysfunctional families are notoriously busy. Homework provides some impetus to focus inward, to reflect on their experiences and to attend to their own needs and development, even when they are not in a group session.

Journaling is a way to develop a baseline of information, a collection of feelings and observations that help individuals learn about the emotions that they may have avoided or denied in the past. It can be painful, as the participants uncover hurt, fear, sadness, or anger that has been hidden or lying dormant.

These exercises are not only powerful group processes, but are valuable methods to stimulate participants to keep exploring and growing between sessions. Written work promotes reflection and helps deepen the learning that takes place during the group meetings.

©1994 Whole Person Press 210 W Michigan Duluth MN 55802   (800) 247-6789

13 CONNECTIONS

Participants examine the ways they begin and end communication with others and learn how to be more effective at both techniques.

GOALS

Examine specific behaviors people use to show interest, understanding, and acceptance of others.

Recognize specific behaviors people use to show their lack of interest and rejection of others.

GROUP SIZE

4 or more

TIME FRAME

30–60 minutes

MATERIALS NEEDED

Copies of handout **How I Connect and Disconnect;** paper and pencils; blackboard or newsprint.

PROCESS

1) The facilitator makes some introductory remarks.

- In dysfunctional families, there is often a large gap between public and private images. These are big differences in the way you present yourself to others and the way you feel inside.

- You may not let people know what you really feel or expect, yet you subtly communicate in ways you may not recognize. You may give mixed messages (i.e., I hear, but I don't want to listen).

- It is important to understand how and what you communicate to others. You can learn to communicate more deliberately and clearly without mixed messages. By becoming more clear and assertive, you feel honest and less frustrated. In return, others often communicate more clearly and respectfully with you.

- When you understand how to connect with and disconnect from people, you can communicate more honestly and directly.

©1994 Whole Person Press 210 W Michigan Duluth MN 55802   (800) 247-6789

2) The facilitator distributes copies of **How I Connect and Disconnect** and asks participants to fill it out, giving the following instructions:

> ➤ Be specific so you can become more aware of your methods of connecting and disconnecting.

> ➤ Don't say "I am bored." Say "I look away," or "I look at my watch."

3) After 10 minutes, the facilitator asks participants to form groups of 4–6 people, writes the following questions on the blackboard or newsprint, and asks participants to discuss them:

> ✔ What are you feeling when you connect or disconnect in these different ways? Do you feel guilty? Impatient? Uncertain?

> ✔ How do others respond to you when you try to connect or when you try to disconnect?

> ✔ What connecting and disconnecting behaviors do you see in your discussion group?

4) The facilitator reconvenes the large group and asks for comments.

> ✔ What are some connect/disconnect messages that you aren't communicating clearly? (The facilitator gives personal examples.)

> ✔ What are some clear ways to give these messages?

> ✔ Why is it hard to be clear? What are the risks and benefits of being more direct in your connect/disconnect messages?

5) The facilitator concludes with the following points:

> • A goal may be to learn more direct ways to state what you want. For example, you might say, "Excuse me, I am interrupting you because I want to leave your office now," rather than sighing and looking at your watch.

> • You connect and disconnect many times each day. When you know how and when you do it, you can communicate directly and clearly and avoid sending mixed messages.

> ☞ *The **Assertiveness** and **Give and Receive Feedback** exercises in the **Healing Patterns** section are good follow-ups to this one.*

HOW I CONNECT AND DISCONNECT

1. Do you make connections by touching people, looking them in the eye, facing them, or leaning towards them? List all the ways you can think of that you connect with other people.

2. Do you disconnect by turning away, or changing the subject when others are talking? List all the ways you can think of that you disconnect with people.

3. How do people usually respond when you connect with them?

4. How do people usually respond when you disconnect from them?

5. List ways you can connect better with others when you choose to.

6. List ways you can disconnect more clearly and assertively.

©1994 Whole Person Press 210 W Michigan Duluth MN 55802   (800) 247-6789

14 OBSESSING

Participants write about, discuss, and visualize an obsessive relationship in their lives and decide how they might free themselves from it.

GOALS

Identify the qualities of an obsessive relationship.

Understand the elements of healthy intimacy.

Identify the importance of detaching from an obsessive relationship.

GROUP SIZE

Unlimited

TIME FRAME

1–2 hours, depending on group size

MATERIALS NEEDED

Copies of **Obsessing Issues;** paper and pencils; blackboard or newsprint.

PROCESS

1) The facilitator introduces the exercise by asking, "What are the similarities and differences between being loved and being needed?" Using the answers to this question, the facilitator presents a brief talk on obsession, making the following points:

   • If you are from a dysfunctional family, you may be likely to choose partners who are needy—an alcoholic, an emotionally withdrawn person, a depressed person who is unable to work at a job. You might choose such a partner, even though you can't count on the partner for any help or cooperation.

   • A needy partner can become an obsession: the only thing you talk or think about. This kind of relationship can interfere with other parts of your life. The obsession becomes so tangled in your head that you can't think or deal with your own problems. You forfeit your power to think, feel, and act for yourself.

2) The facilitator asks the following questions:

✔ What are some obsessive relationships you know about, either from personal experience or from the media?

✔ What are the obsessing persons getting out of the relationships?

✔ In what ways are they not taking care of themselves or others because of this obsession?

3) The facilitator distributes copies of **Obsessing Issues,** and blank paper and asks participants to write a paragraph in response to each question. (10 minutes)

4) The facilitator outlines several points about detaching from unhealthy obsessions.

- You can get over an obsession and begin a healthier relationship, even with the person you are *obsessing* over.

- Real intimacy means learning to care about someone else, without feeling that it is your role to fix, and change, and do everything for that person. You can learn to do this, but first you have to *detach* yourself from this other person.

- Al-Anon describes detachment as "mentally, emotionally and sometimes physically disengaging yourself from unhealthy entanglements with another person's life and responsibilities, and from problems you cannot solve."

5) The facilitator asks participants to form groups of 3–4 members and discuss the questions listed below. She writes a question on the blackboard or newsprint and has the groups discuss it for 5 minutes before writing the next question.

✔ What did you say in your **Obsessing Issues** writing exercise?

✔ How do you feel about detaching from that person?

✔ What will happen if you detach?

✔ What will happen if you don't detach?

✔ How has staying attached helped you so far?

6) The facilitator asks participants to write for 3–5 minutes on the topic: "If this person were not in my life, what would I be doing today?"

7) The facilitator leads the participants through the following visualization, pausing for a minute or so after each paragraph. (5–10 minutes)

We are going to try to visualize as clearly as possible what life without this person would be like.

I would like you to get comfortable, either in your chair or on the floor. Close your eyes and think about the person that you are so strongly attached to. How do you feel when you think about this person? Does the thought give you pleasure? Pain? (pause)

Imagine now that this person is leaving your life. Starting with this moment, you will no longer see or talk to this person. Everything belonging to this person will be gone, too. You can't drive by this person's home or call him or her on the telephone. (pause)

Now that this person is gone, how do you feel? Are you afraid? Glad? Angry? Sad? Identify the dominant feeling, then let all the other feelings come in too. (pause)

What will you do with your free time now that this person is gone? Starting from the time you get up in the morning . . . when you go to work . . . all day long . . . in the evening . . . and when you go to bed at night. How will your day be different now? (pause)

Who will you spend your time with? (pause)

What can you do now that you couldn't do with the person in your life? (pause)

Slowly open your eyes and stretch. Look around and notice your surroundings.

8) The facilitator asks participants to write down two small things that they will do to detach from this person in their life. She gives some examples, such as, "I will not drive by her house each day," or "When he is watching TV, I will no longer check on him every 30 minutes to see if he needs something."

©1994 Whole Person Press 210 W Michigan Duluth MN 55802   (800) 247-6789

OBSESSING ISSUES

1. Write about a person in your life who you are excessively attached to or worried about. Write as much as you can.

John drives me crazy. I worry about him all the time. I don't know what to expect next. He says that he will be home at 6:00 and he doesn't come home until 10:00, usually drunk. He says he stopped off at the tavern to say hello to a friend and lost track of time. Well, he drinks too much and I try not to nag him, but what if he has an accident, or kills someone, or falls down and hurts himself? The kids get so hurt when he doesn't show up to see their softball games. He says he can't get away from work, but he has enough time to go to the tavern.

2. After you have written as much as you can about this person, now focus on yourself. Write only about how you feel and what you think concerning this person. Start each sentence with "I feel . . . " or "I think . . . "

I am scared, scared of losing John, of not having security, of the kids being hurt, of me staying lonely. I don't feel safe. I am embarrassed, worried that others will think badly of me and my family. I am angry, angry that I cannot count on John, that I need him, that I am dependent on him, that I can't make him stop drinking. I feel trapped. I am sad, for the lost good times, for being lonely without a partner to talk with. I want to cry all the time.

©1994 Whole Person Press 210 W Michigan Duluth MN 55802   (800) 247-6789

15 DISTRACTION FROM FEELINGS

Participants write and talk about the ways they avoid dealing with their feelings and how they can face their feelings more successfully.

GOALS

Identify the ways in which feelings are avoided and denied.

Develop new strategies for attending to feelings.

Learn how to minimize "distractions" that are used to avoid feelings.

GROUP SIZE

Unlimited

TIME FRAME

30–45 minutes

MATERIALS NEEDED

Paper and pencils; blackboard or newsprint.

PROCESS

1) The facilitator introduces the exercise by making the following comments:

   - Our culture struggles with addiction. Addictions are most often convenient ways to distract yourself from or to help deny painful feelings.

   - Some of the most common addictive agents are:

alcohol	jogging	illegal drugs	cults
reading	speed	gambling	danger
nicotine	food	relationships	sex
caffeine	power	television	work
spending	stress	prescription drugs	

   - These agents are not always addictions. It is their abuse that leads to addiction. It is the lack of moderation that creates the problem.

- When these substances or behaviors are excessively used to avoid or deny your feelings of intimacy, inner torment, insecurity, or other problems, they become the basis for addiction.

- Addiction is over-extended involvement with the agent or activity. The addictive process can take many forms, and always includes elements of avoidance and denial.

- The addicted person may seem in control, but that is an illusion.

- When you are doing something to avoid or deny feelings, you are not in control of your life. The agent that you are using to protect yourself from your feelings is in control of your life.

- The "don't rock the boat" rule of the family can be the internal rule for an organization or society as well. In order to keep the boat steady, it appears to be critically important not to let the feelings, pain, and problems surface.

- The behavior that is used to hide the pain becomes an addiction: drinking, gambling, working, cleaning, taking care of someone else, exercising, or taking excessive risks.

- There is a cultural encouragement for this kind of over-extension. For example, television advertisements show only happy, beautiful, trouble-free people drinking alcohol in bars; corporations reward employees who work 50–60 hours per week; the aerobic gods and goddesses of exercise encourage you to look like them.

2) The facilitator makes comments about distracting activities that can be used to avoid real feelings. Examples of distractions include

fast talking	cleaning	shopping
watching TV	reading	sleeping
eating	nagging	having a drink
blaming	telephoning	talking about people

asking about others to avoid talking about yourself

3) The facilitator gives the following instructions:

➤ Think about times when you are sad, mad, or hurt.

➤ Write down some of the ways you try to avoid these feelings, calm yourself down, and get control of yourself again. Could any of these become addictive?

4) After 3 minutes, the facilitator writes the following questions on the blackboard or newsprint and asks participants to form groups of 4–5 people to discuss the questions.

✔ What distractions do you use?

✔ How often do you use a distraction?

✔ What else could you do to allow your feelings to be felt and let go of your protections?

✔ How could you moderate your distractions?

5) The facilitator reconvenes the large group and asks participants to report on one way they will moderate their distractions.

TRAINER'S NOTES

16 SHAMEFUL FEELINGS

This exercise uses a worksheet and a vocabulary of "feeling words" for explaining the concept of shame and learning to deal with it.

GOALS

Acknowledge specific events or circumstances that have caused feelings of shame.

Identify specific mistakes that cause the shame.

Experience the difference between shame and acknowledging a mistake.

GROUP SIZE

Unlimited

TIME FRAME

30–50 minutes for discussion

MATERIALS NEEDED

Paper, pencils, and copies of the **Shameful Feelings** worksheet and the **Feeling Words Vocabulary** list.

☞ *Although this exercise can be completed in 1 session, it is effective to have participants complete Step 1 between sessions.*

PROCESS

☞ *It can be frightening to admit shameful feelings, and to experience shame and embarrassment again or for the first time. Provide privacy for participants to write.*

1) The facilitator distributes the **Shameful Feelings** worksheet and asks participants to complete Part A. (10 minutes)

2) The facilitator distributes the **Feeling Words Vocabulary** list and asks participants to use this list to complete Part B of the **Shameful Feelings** worksheet. (5–8 minutes)

3) The facilitator asks participants to form groups of 4–5 and gives these instructions:

➤ Talk about the experience of making the Part B list. What was it like to identify the shame and associated feelings?

➤ Focus on the feelings that this exercise brings to light, rather than on the event you are ashamed of. Consult the **Feeling Words Vocabulary** to help you label the feelings.

➤ Share and listen to each other. Accept what others say. Do not try to rescue them or help them feel better.

4) The participants remain in small groups and the facilitator makes these points about shame:

- When you feel shame you may believe that you are a mistake.

- Deep levels of shame may come from being consistently invalidated or discounted in your family.

- These feelings may begin because of physical, emotional, or sexual abuse. Self-destruction and self-loathing may follow.

- Feelings of shame may be related to a secret, such as getting pregnant as a teenager.

- When you experience shame regularly, you may also experience isolation, perfectionism, depression, compulsions (eating, spending, sexual activity, cleaning, etc.), or eating disorders. Life can be a constant struggle.

5) With the participants still in small groups, the facilitator gives the following instructions:

➤ Look at the list of events that make you feel ashamed (Part A).

➤ Now complete Part C of **Shameful Feelings.**

6) After 5–8 minutes, the facilitator gives participants these instructions:

➤ Choose 1 mistake from Part C and tell it to your group.

➤ Start each phrase with, "I made a mistake and it was . . ." and end it with, "I am a good person and I make mistakes."

☞ *For a graphic explanation of shame, refer to the* **Model of Dysfunctional Patterns** *in the* **Self-Esteem** *exercise in the* **Taking Stock** *section.*

©1994 Whole Person Press 210 W Michigan Duluth MN 55802   (800) 247-6789

FEELING WORDS VOCABULARY

STRONG INTENSITY				
HAPPY	SAD	ANGRY	SCARED	CONFUSED
Excited	Hopeless	Furious	Fearful	Bewildered
Elated	Sorrowful	Seething	Panicky	Trapped
Exuberant	Depressed	Enraged	Afraid	Troubled
Ecstatic	Wounded	Hostile	Shocked	Demobilized
Terrific	Hurt	Vengeful	Overwhelmed	Stagnant
Jubilant	Drained	Incensed	Startled	Ambivalent
Alive	Defeated	Abused	Intimidated	
Energized	Exhausted	Hateful	Desperate	
Enthusiastic	Helpless	Humiliated	Frantic	
Loved	Crushed	Sabotaged	Terrified	
	Worthless	Betrayed	Vulnerable	
	Uncared for	Repulsed		
	Dejected	Jealous		
	Rejected	Pissed off		
	Empty	Bitter		
	Miserable			
	Distraught			

MODERATE INTENSITY				
HAPPY	SAD	ANGRY	SCARED	CONFUSED
Valued	Disappointed	Resentful	Tense	Awkward
Gratified	Upset	Disgusted	Threatened	Puzzled
Encouraged	Inadequate	Smothered	Uneasy	Disoriented
Optimistic	Dismal	Frustrated	Defensive	Foggy
Joyful	Unappreciated	Stifled	Insecure	
Proud	Discouraged	Offended	Skeptical	
Cheerful	Ashamed	Infantilized	Apprehensive	
Relieved	Distressed	Controlled	Suspicious	
Assured	Distant	Peeved	Perturbed	
Determined	Disillusioned	Annoyed		
Grateful	Lonely	Agitated		
Appreciated	Isolated	Irritated		
Confident	Alienated			
Respected	Abandoned			
Admired	Regretful			
Accepted				

MILD INTENSITY				
HAPPY	SAD	ANGRY	SCARED	CONFUSED
Content	Sorry	Uptight	Reluctant	Bothered
Relaxed	Lost	Dismayed	Anxious	Undecided
Glad	Bad	Tolerant	Shy	Uncomfortable
Good		Resigned	Nervous	Perplexed
Satisfied			Unsure	
Peaceful			Timid	
Calm			Concerned	
Tranquil			Doubtful	
Hopeful			Worried	
Enjoyable				
Pleased				
Relieved				
Hoping to be great				
Looking forward				

©1994 Whole Person Press 210 W Michigan Duluth MN 55802   (800) 247-6789

SHAMEFUL FEELINGS

A. List 5 events or experiences from your life of which you are ashamed.

1.

2.

3.

4.

5.

B. Using the **Feelings Words Vocabulary** write in the word or words that describe your feelings about each shameful event from Part A.

Event	Happy	Sad	Angry	Scared	Confused
1					
2					
3					
4					
5					

C. Look at the items you listed in Part A, and rephrase them, acknowledging that they were mistakes.

1.

2.

3.

4.

5.

17 GUILT LIST

Through writing and discussion, participants analyze guilt feelings and assess their levels of control and responsibility.

GOALS

Identify specific situations or events that cause feelings of guilt.

Analyze the degree of control and responsibility one has over the situations that cause guilt.

Develop strategies for decreasing guilty feelings.

GROUP SIZE

Unlimited

TIME FRAME

45–60 minutes

MATERIALS NEEDED

Blackboard or newsprint; blank paper and pencils.

PROCESS

1) The facilitator introduces the exercise by making the following points:

   • People from severely dysfunctional families are *chronic self-doubt-ers.*

   • When you feel guilt you may say to yourself, "I made a mistake," or you may say "I can never be good enough," "I can never do anything right," or "I will never please him."

   • You may take responsibility for the mistakes of others without considering where the responsibility really lies. You may say, "I'm sorry" a lot. You may assume all mistakes are your fault, so you automatically apologize. In extreme cases you may even begin to apologize for being alive.

2) The facilitator gives participants the following instructions:

   ➤ Take 5 minutes and write down all the situations or events about which you currently feel guilty.

➤ Now decide which ones you have some control over. Cross out those over which you have no control—and therefore have no need to feel guilty about.

3) The facilitator asks participants to form groups of 3 people and discuss these questions written on the blackboard or newsprint.

✔ What did it feel like to make the guilt list?

✔ How did you decide whether you had control?

✔ What were your feelings when you crossed out the items that you cannot control?

✔ How will you remind yourself that you do not always have control?

4) The facilitator reconvenes the large group and asks participants to call out phrases people use when they feel guilty, mentioning the following examples if they are not brought up by the group: "I'm sorry," "I wish I could help, but I don't know how," "It's my fault," "You're right, I'm wrong," "How could I be so stupid?" "What is wrong with me?" "Why can't I ever get this right?" "What a dope I am," "Why didn't I think of that?" "What did I do *now*?"

5) The facilitator lists the following tips for dealing with appropriate guilt and writes them on the blackboard or newsprint.

● Say to yourself, "I'm doing the best I can."

● Be a mirror, not a sponge. When others blame you, reflect their feeling—saying, for instance, "You're angry at me," or "You are upset"—rather than accepting the blame.

● Remind yourself that you have limits (time, energy, resources) and that self-care is also a responsibility.

● Keep a shoe box in your closet where you can store guilt whenever you feel it. Imagine yourself opening the lid, dumping new guilt in, and then slamming the lid shut before any escapes!

6) The facilitator asks participants to give other ideas for decreasing guilt and adds them to the list.

18 MANAGING AND CONTROLLING

This writing and discussion exercise ends with a meditation to help participants moderate their anxiety about control, and to help them practice "letting go."

GOALS

Identify the people or situations that are the focus of managing and controlling behaviors.

Assess the consequences of managing and controlling behaviors.

Use meditation and music to reduce anxiety over control.

GROUP SIZE

Unlimited

TIME FRAME

45–60 minutes

MATERIALS NEEDED

Paper and pencils; copies of **Managing and Controlling Assessment** and **Managing and Controlling Questions**; blackboard or newsprint; cassette tape of meditation music; cassette player.

PROCESS

1) The facilitator gives a short chalktalk making the following points:

- When you attempt to control people and events that you have no business controlling you forfeit your power to think, feel, and act in accordance with your own best interests.

- You frequently lose control of yourself. You are being controlled not just by people, but by addictive behaviors, such as eating disorders, compulsive spending, cleaning, or talking.

- You cannot change people. They will resist your efforts to change them and may double their own efforts to prove they can't be controlled. No amount of control will effect a permanent or desirable change in another person. The only person you can change is yourself. The only person you should attempt to control is yourself.

2) The facilitator distributes the **Managing and Controlling Questions** and asks participants to fill it out. (5–8 minutes)

3) The facilitator asks participants to form groups of 4–6 people, instructing each group to choose one example from the **Managing and Controlling Questions** worksheet and to then discuss the following questions written on the newsprint or blackboard:

   ✔ How do you benefit from attempting to control the situation?

   ✔ How does the other person benefit from your attempts to control the situation?

   ✔ How effective are your attempts at controlling the outcome of events?

4) The facilitator distributes the **Managing and Controlling Assessment** and asks participants to place an X at the appropriate place on the line beneath each question. (3–5 minutes)

5) The facilitator reconvenes the large group and leads a discussion, using the following questions:

   ✔ What are the most common ways in which you try to control people?

   ✔ When does control or the lack of it make you the most anxious?

6) The facilitator gives a brief chalktalk.

   • Controlling people takes a lot of effort and is usually not successful anyway! When control makes you anxious concentrate on relaxing, not on getting better at controlling.

   • Anxiety can be reduced by using relaxation techniques.

   • We are going to try a simple exercise you can use to deal with anxiety.

7) The facilitator starts playing the cassette tape of relaxing music and asks participants to breathe deeply and to silently repeat this phrase as they exhale: "Everything will be all right." The facilitator reminds participants to breathe deeply during the exercise. (3 minutes)

   ☞ *This is an emotionally calming and physically relaxing activity that helps participants accept the flow of life without the need for hyper-vigilance. Encourage participants to use this relaxation technique frequently. They may choose a different phrase that fits their life.*

Some suggested music:

> *Autumn* (1980) or *Winter into Spring* (1980) by George Winston, Windham Hill Records. Piano solos that can soothe the soul.

> *A Feather on the Breath of God*, sequences and hymns by Abbess Hildegard of Bingen (1179). Hyperion Records Limited, London, England, Phonographic Performance Ltd., Ganton House, 14-22 Ganton Street, London, W1V, lLB, England. This Gothic music is sacred. It can make you want to pray and dance at the same time.

> *Prelude,* Steven Halpern, Halpern Sounds, 1175 Old Country Road #9, Belmont, CA 94002. Lovely meditation music.

> ☞ *The **Obsessing** exercise in this section has more about the issue of detachment, and it makes a good follow-up to this one.*

TRAINER'S NOTES

MANAGING AND CONTROLLING QUESTIONS

1. Make a list of the people and events you are trying to control. List as many as you can.

2. Choose one of your examples above. Write about how you feel controlled (mentally, emotionally, or physically) by what or whom you are attempting to control.

3. What would happen (to you and the other person) if you detached and became less controlling?

4. What will probably happen anyway, in spite of your controlling efforts?

©1994 Whole Person Press 210 W Michigan Duluth MN 55802   (800) 247-6789

MANAGING AND CONTROLLING ASSESSMENT

1. I am afraid to let others be who they are.

Never   Sometimes   Always

2. I am afraid to let events happen naturally.

Never   Sometimes   Always

3. I fear losing control.

Never   Sometimes   Always

4. I think I know best how things should turn out and how others should behave.

Never   Sometimes   Always

5. I try to control events and people through helplessness, guilt, coercion, or threats.

Never   Sometimes   Always

6. I try to control events and people through advice-giving, manipulation, or domination.

Never   Sometimes   Always

7. I get frustrated and angry when others don't do things my way.

Never   Sometimes   Always

8. I feel controlled by events and people.

Never   Sometimes   Always

9. I am afraid to let others know who I am.

Never   Sometimes   Always

19 MOURNING YOUR LOSSES

Participants write about and discuss small and large losses, and how to grieve in helpful, healing ways.

GOALS

Identify personal losses.

Assess the effects of the past losses on present-day life.

Experience the positive effects of grieving.

GROUP SIZE

Unlimited

TIME FRAME

60–75 minutes

MATERIALS NEEDED

Copies of the **Problems When a Loss is Experienced** and **The Grief Process** worksheets; a 20–30 minute video segment dealing with loss. Suggestions for rentable movies include: *Old Yeller, Charlotte's Web, Ordinary People, The Prince of Tides, Terms of Endearment, Steel Magnolias, The Bear,* and *Rocket Gibraltar.* A video that shows characters dealing with the loss of a loved one or the loss of innocence is recommended. Review these movies and pick a segment that demonstrates the grieving process. Suggestions for 20–minute (without commercials) situation comedies that you can videotape in advance include: *M*A*S*H, Designing Women, Empty Nest, Golden Girls.*

PROCESS

1) The facilitator shows a video as an aid for bringing feelings and memories to the surface.

2) The facilitator gives a short chalktalk about losses.

   • Even with small losses your feelings may be intense.

   • Losses may focus on a person, an object, or an event— for example, the death of your grandmother, the lost opportunity for further education, the death of your dog, moving away from a friend when you were a child, or a divorce.

- Loss can be less concrete, such as loss of innocence when you realized there was no tooth fairy, or when you realized a beloved relative might hurt you. A 12-year-old girl, for example, lost her mother as a confidant when her mother told her, "If you do something that you know I won't like, don't tell me." She believed her mother, and stopped talking to her about important events and emotions for fear that she would upset her. This was an intense loss at the beginning of puberty.

3) The facilitator gives the following instructions:

➤ Write out all the losses you can think of from your life. (10 minutes)

➤ Record small, abstract losses, as well as major life events.

4) The facilitator distributes **The Grief Process** worksheet, reviews the phases, and makes the following points:

- Grieving for a loss is a natural healing experience.

- The grief process can be short or can take place over years.

- You can move from phase to phase and then back to a previous phase. The movement is not always sequential or predictable.

- Having the feelings, without attempting to hide or control them, is the healthiest way to experience the grief process.

5) The facilitator writes the following questions on the blackboard or newsprint and then asks participants to form groups of 3 people to discuss the questions.*

✔ Because of my accumulation of losses (which I have written down), what opportunities were stolen from me?

✔ What normal growing-up experiences did I miss?

✔ What relationships have I lost?

✔ What dreams and visions was I forced to give up because of tip-toeing around someone in the family?

✔ What areas of my life are less fulfilling today because of what happened to me?

✔ What phase of the grieving process am I in for each major loss?

©1994 Whole Person Press 210 W Michigan Duluth MN 55802   (800) 247-6789

☞ *People may cry, shake, become angry, or feel scared as they recall some of these memories. Be ready to listen. Ask group members to listen and give support and validation.*

6) The facilitator distributes the **Problems When a Loss is Experienced** worksheet and asks participants to complete it. (3 minutes)

7) The facilitator makes the following comments:

- Learn to recognize the signs of grieving and the resulting problems when the process of grieving is short circuited.

- Accept the feelings that come with grief. They are a critical component in healing.

- Talking with others about these feelings and problems is helpful in the grieving process.

TRAINER'S NOTES

Questions in Step 5 taken from The Courage to Heal Workbook, *Ellen Bass and Laura Davis, ©1988 by Ellen Bass and Laura Davis. Reprinted with permission of HarperCollins Publishers.*

THE GRIEF PROCESS

If you are grieving, set aside some time each day to express it. This will make it easier to accept the feelings at other times.

Denial
> You may experience a sense of numbness.
> You may repeat phrases, such as, "This didn't happen. It's a bad dream."

Anger
> You may be angry at a person or situation, or at everything.
> You may be angry with yourself.

Bargaining
> You would do or offer anything to get the person back or to change the situation.

Depression
> You feel blah.
> You may ask: "What is the purpose of life?" or you may say "Who cares," to everything.

Acceptance
> You begin to feel free of emotional pain and are less invested in the past relationship or state of innocence.

PROBLEMS WHEN A LOSS IS EXPERIENCED

Mark whether or not you have experienced the following problems in your grieving process.

	Yes	No
Sleeplessness		
Fatigue		
Change in eating patterns		
Sighing—release of body tension		
Rapid mood change		
Sense of loss of reality—feeling dazed or detached		
Lack of contact with emotions		
Fantasizing		
Loneliness		
Lack of concentration		
Weakness and helplessness		
Depression		
Guilt		
Lack of interest in sex		
Self-criticism		
Anger		
Suicidal feelings		
Physical symptoms—headaches, colitis		
Constant talking that drives others away		

20 PUBLIC VS. PRIVATE SELF

Drawing with crayons, participants examine the differences between their public and private masks.

GOALS

Clarify the difference between how participants try to appear to others and how they feel about themselves.

Release tension to allow sharing of the internal view of self.

GROUP SIZE

Unlimited

TIME FRAME

30–45 minutes

MATERIALS NEEDED

Paper, crayons of many colors, and pencils; blackboard or newsprint.

PROCESS

1) The facilitator gives the following instructions:

> ➤ Take your paper and crayons and draw a mask of the face that you usually present to others, your public face. Use the whole paper for your drawing.

> ➤ Use colors, sizes and details that represent the way you think you present yourself.

> ➤ This is not a competitive exercise, but a way to show how you believe you present yourself to the outside world.

> ➤ You have 10–15 minutes to work, so spend some time thinking about your drawing before you start

2) The facilitator draws his own masks.

3) After participants finish their public masks, the facilitator gives them the following instructions:

> ➤ Now I want you to turn the paper over and draw a picture or mask of your real self, the self you don't show to the public.

➤ Include the beauty and the blemishes, the way you feel you really are.

➤ Once again take 10–15 minutes to do this.

4) The facilitator shows the group his public mask and describes it. Then he turns the paper around and shows his "private mask."

☞ *If you like, describe some of it as well. (Note: Share only what you wish!)*

5) The facilitator asks participants to form groups of 4–6 people for discussion. He writes the following questions on the blackboard or newsprint:

✔ What details did you draw, and what do they mean?

✔ What did you knowingly leave out of the first mask?

✔ What percentage of your personality is represented by each mask?

✔ Who sees or knows the private mask, besides you?

6) After 15–20 minutes, the facilitator reconvenes the large group and asks for insights and comments about how people reveal themselves to others.

TRAINER'S NOTES

©1994 Whole Person Press 210 W Michigan Duluth MN 55802   (800) 247-6789

21 FEELING CARDS

Participants maintain a week-long record of their feelings and analyze the record for meaningful patterns.

GOALS

Acquire a structure for recognizing and understanding your feelings.

See the patterns that occur in feelings.

Gain hope for behavior change.

GROUP SIZE

Unlimited

TIME FRAME

20–40 minutes for discussion

MATERIALS NEEDED

Copies of the **Feeling Words Vocabulary** (in the **Shameful Feelings** exercise in this section), the **Feeling Card Examples,** and the **Feeling Cards Chart.**

> ☞ *This exercise is best used in two sessions: one to get people started with their records and the other to conduct a group discussion. If the facilitator does not want to conduct the discussion or only meets with the group once, the assignment can still be made. Participants who are motivated will complete the exercise on their own.*

PROCESS

1) The facilitator distributes copies of the **Feeling Cards Examples,** the **Feeling Words Vocabulary,** and the **Feeling Cards Chart.**

2) The facilitator gives the following instructions:

➤ I want you to get a package of index cards and to carry a card and pencil with you each day.

➤ Date a new card each day and ask yourself 15 times throughout the day, "How am I feeling right now?" Whatever the feeling is, write it on the card and mark the time. Consult the **Feeling Cards Examples** to see examples.

➤ Use the **Feeling Words Vocabulary** to help you clarify feelings.

➤ Keep the cards private, and keep them in order by date.

➤ Just before our next session look at your collection of cards. Use the **Feeling Cards Chart** to make notes about patterns you see. The patterns may reveal dominant feelings or changes at certain times of the day.

➤ Come to the next session ready to discuss what you learned about yourself.

3) At the next session, the facilitator asks participants to form groups of 4–5 and to discuss the following questions, which she has written on the blackboard or newsprint:

✔ What is the most common feeling category (Happy, Sad, Angry, Scared, Confused) on your **Feeling Cards Chart?**

✔ Now that you are more aware of your feelings, what would you change about what you do or say to others?

✔ How can you maintain this awareness of your feelings?

✔ What usually keeps you from knowing your feelings?

4) To end the exercise, the facilitator reconvenes the group and makes the following points:

● Some people report that after writing feeling cards for a week, they realize that they often do not know how they feel. This is a common experience for people raised in dysfunctional families.

● This exercise can become a life-long habit. You can ask yourself several times a day, "How am I feeling right now?"

● The more you ask, the easier it will be to know. Since much of your life may have been spent denying or avoiding your feelings, it takes time to learn to listen to your inner voice.

● As you begin to recognize how you feel, you may experience feelings of anger or sadness. You may want to distance yourself from these feelings, but it is important that you keep asking yourself about feelings and allowing yourself time each day to deal with the sadness, anger, and other feelings.

- Look for patterns. For example, you may have a low time at 3:00 or 4:00P.M. each day. This can be related to inconsistent eating patterns, perhaps missing breakfast and/or lunch, or some other circumstance.

- You may ask yourself, "Why would I want to know these angry or sad feelings?" First, in order to feel emotionally intimate with others, you must be able to share your feelings with another who will listen. If you don't know your feelings, then you can't share them. This is lonely and isolating. Also, when you know how you feel, you have choices about what you will do or how you will react. These choices are freeing. It is limiting to have unexpressed feelings that can lead to "tolerance breaks" or angry blow ups.

  ☞ *See the exercise* **Trash Compactor** *in the* **Healing Patterns** *section for more about storing feelings.*

TRAINER'S NOTES

FEELING CARDS EXAMPLES

1/17

9 am / Scared about boss being disappointed with me.

10:30 am /Mad, Sally did not tell me that I needed to stay over lunch.

1 pm / Happy, remembering the sweet things that Joe said last night.

1/18

8 am / Sad, thinking about the good times I used to have with my sisters, who have all moved away.

Noon / I am so mad at the situation at work, and I can't seem to say what I want to Jerry.

7 pm / Geez, I am so tired and frustrated that I cannot find time for myself.

1/19

6:30 am / Woke up worried that I would not remember to take the chicken out of the freezer, then mad that no one appreciates it anyway.

10 am / Embarrassed that I did not remember Ellen's birthday and others did.

3 pm / Today, I have been so off balance and unfocused, and confused about what I feel most of the time.

FEELING CARDS CHART

Days	Happy	Sad	Angry	Scared	Confused
1					
2					
3					
4					
5					
6					
7					
8					
9					
10					
11					
12					
13					
14					

What patterns do you see?

Healing Patterns

HEALING PATTERNS

HEALING PATTERNS

Even when old patterns cause pain, change can be very frightening. There will be many group participants who both want to change and are afraid to change. In her book *Dance of Intimacy*, Harriet Lerner confirms this understanding of change:

> You can count on only two things that will never change. What will never change is the will to change and the fear to change. It is the will to change that motivates us to seek help. It is the fear of change that motivates us to resist the very help we seek.

Yet, because dysfunctional patterns are learned, they can be unlearned. Behavior can be changed so that life can be more satisfying and rewarding. However, recovery from dysfunctional patterns requires lifelong attention to the behaviors that need changing.

It's okay to change the "rules" that were learned in dysfunctional families. Most successful recovery programs, such as counseling, Adult Children support groups, or twelve-step programs, are based on the reality that change is possible, with the right approach and support.

Two concepts are important in regard to change:

1. Go slow and think small.
2. There is no perfection, but rather progress.

Small and steady progress can help people to repattern their relational style. There is no end of the line, no absolute healing. The healing process is the beginning of a lifelong growth that consists of paying attention to oneself and making choices based on self-knowledge.

The exercises in this section will help participants pay attention to their own feelings, and in the process, build the self-knowledge that is the basis of all successful change.

22 MY LOVES

In this enjoyable exercise, participants make a written "Contract to Do What I Love."

GOALS

Identify 15 favorite activities.

Make a written commitment to doing two of the favorite activities.

GROUP SIZE

8 or more

TIME FRAME

30–40 minutes

MATERIALS NEEDED

Paper and pencils; copies of **Contract To Do What I Love;** blackboard or newsprint.

PROCESS

1) The facilitator gives participants the following instructions:

   ➤ Take 5 minutes and write down 15 activities that you love. These activities can be simple or complex. Examples may include taking a hot bath in the evening, traveling to Japan, working in the garden, reading in the morning before anyone else is up, or walking with a friend in the woods.

   ➤ Each item should be specific. Write down activities that are doable and verifiable.

2) After participants have written for 5 minutes, the facilitator gives the following instructions:

   ➤ Circle 2 items from your list that you will do or take steps toward doing within one week.

   ➤ If the activity cannot be completed within one week, list one or more steps that you will take during the next week.

3) The facilitator distributes the **Contract To Do What I Love** and fills out a personal sample contract on the blackboard or newsprint. The facilitator then gives these instructions:

➤ Fill out the steps you will take during the next week to do the 2 activities that you circled.

➤ This contract should be specific about when and how you will accomplish these activities.

➤ If you find it difficult to make this commitment, remember, the responsibility is to yourself.

4) The facilitator asks participants to form groups of 2-3 people and gives these instructions:

➤ Share your written contract with others in your group.

➤ Make sure that the contracts are specific, that they can be accomplished and that there would be a way of verifying they have been done.

5) The facilitator concludes by making a few points:

● Long-term change is not quick. Go slow and think small.

● You heal when you treat yourself—and allow yourself to do something you love to do!

● This exercise is one that you can do for yourself at any time.

● Try to do something you love at least once a week.

TRAINER'S NOTES

CONTRACT TO DO WHAT I LOVE

I would love to _____ . I agree to take
the following steps to accomplish it.

By _____ I will do the following:

_____

_____

_____

_____

_____

and by _____ I will do the following:

_____

_____

_____

_____

_____

_____   _____
  Signature   Date

23 BEFRIENDING YOUR CHILD

Through listening to a story, participants fantasize about a childhood experience and become more aware of their "child" selves.

GOALS

Fantasize about meeting yourself as a child.

Experience feelings of love and nurturance for the child-self.

Identify and discuss ways to nurture the child-self in everyday life.

GROUP SIZE

6 or more

TIME FRAME

45–60 minutes

MATERIALS NEEDED

Copies of the **Reaction to Befriending Your Child** worksheet; gong, or drum and bell; quiet room where participants can comfortably lie on the floor.

PROCESS

1) The facilitator introduces the exercise by explaining that participants will become more aware of their "child" selves by fantasizing about a childhood experience.

2) The facilitator gives the following instructions:

   ➤ Get in a comfortable position. You may be more comfortable sitting in a chair, or you may want to lie or sit on the floor.

   ➤ Close your eyes.

   ➤ Breathe deeply.

   ➤ Concentrate on the air going in and out of your nose.

   ➤ Ignore other sounds around you.

   ➤ Listen carefully to the story that I will read.

➤ When I stop reading, imagine your child coming to you.

➤ During the time you are with your child, I will sound a drum (or gong) about every 30 seconds.

➤ A bell will ring to indicate the end of the fantasy.

3) The facilitator reads the fantasy very slowly and clearly. The facilitator should also be breathing regularly and deeply.

    ☞ *Some trainers find it easier to put this step on tape.*

Sitting with your eyes closed, breathe deeply, following your breath in and out.

There still exists in your being, yourself as a child, a child who does not know that in some other time frame of its existence he or she has grown up.

As the drum (or gong) sounds, call upon this child to come forward from wherever he or she exists. You might even want to open your right hand so you can be reached by your child.

The child, who was yourself, may appear during the sounding of the drum (or gong) or may appear at the end of the sounds. In either case, as soon as you feel your child's presence, be attentive to the child.

You want to do this with your active imagination. You may want to imagine rocking the child or walking around with her or him, and imagine being very active, during this time. Find the way that seems appropriate for you.

You may find that you actually feel in your right hand a little hand holding yours. Feel the needs and personality of this child. If your child is willing, hold your child in your arms.

Talk with your child. Walk with him or her. Take this child, if you like, to some place like the circus or the beach or the zoo, or let the child take you somewhere. Play with this child who was you.

Give love, friendship, nurturing to the child, and allow yourself to receive from the child, who has as much, if not more, to offer you. You have fifteen minutes to begin the friendship with yourself as a child.

You will be called back to the present by the ringing of a bell.

©1994 Whole Person Press 210 W Michigan Duluth MN 55802   (800) 247-6789

4) When the story is finished the facilitator begins to sound the drum (or gong) every 30 seconds for 15 minutes. The facilitator should remain very quiet, allowing participants to imagine their own befriending.

5) After sounding the bell to signal the end of the fantasy, the facilitator gives the following instructions:

➤ Keep breathing deeply, and slowly open your eyes.

➤ Come back to the present.

6) After most participants have opened their eyes, the facilitator quietly distributes the **Reaction to Befriending Your Child** worksheet and asks participants to write about their experience. (10 minutes)

7) The facilitator places the participants in groups of 2–3 people, and gives the following instructions:

> ☞ *Placing participants in groups for the discussion, rather than letting them decide where to sit, allows them to stay with their child and not be required to make decisions.*

➤ Bring your child with you so that you can share this experience with other people in the group.

➤ Bring your **Reaction to Befriending Your Child** worksheet with you also.

➤ Allow your "child" self to talk and act through you as you share your adult consciousness.

➤ Using your **Reaction to Befriending Your Child** worksheet, share your responses with others in your group.

TRAINER'S NOTES

Befriending Your Child reading adapted from The Possible Human, *Jean Houston, ©1982, Jeremy P. Tarcher, Inc., Los Angeles, CA.*

REACTION TO BEFRIENDING YOUR CHILD

How old is your child in your fantasy?

What did you do with your child during the fantasy?
Hold her/his hand? Take a walk? Listen to her/him?

What feelings did you have during your fantasy?

How can you continue to nurture and love your child in your life?

What other reactions do you have to spending time with your child?

24 GIVE AND RECEIVE FEEDBACK

Through chalktalks, handouts, and interaction with other group members, participants learn and practice non-judgmental feedback skills.

GOALS

Understand the guidelines for giving and receiving non-judgmental feedback.

Practice giving and receiving non-judgmental feedback.

GROUP SIZE

6–10

TIME FRAME

80–140 minutes

MATERIALS NEEDED

Pencils and copies of the **Guidelines for Giving and Receiving Feedback, Examples of Active Awareness and Feedback,** and **Feedback Yes, Interpretation No** worksheets.

PROCESS

1) The facilitator distributes the **Examples of Active Awareness and Feedback** worksheets and makes the following points:

- This exercise provides valuable information about how you give and receive feedback. It also allows time for you to practice your feedback skills.

- In the **Examples of Active Awareness and Feedback** worksheets you can see that giving feedback focuses on making observations, not on making judgements or giving advice.

- With feedback, you say, "I noticed that you . . . " With judgments you say, "I like how you did that . . . " With advice, you say, "Why don't you try . . . "

- Good feedback gives information that others can interpret for themselves. Its purpose is not to fix problems, give solutions, or tell another what to do.

- The use of "I statements" is particularly useful in giving feedback. For example, saying, "I feel scared when you scream," or "I am confused by what you said," puts ownership of the feeling squarely with the speaker. "You" statements, such as "You scare me" or "You are confusing," imply that another person is responsible for your feelings.

- Giving feedback is a valuable interpersonal skill. It is a way of helping other people understand how their behavior is interpreted by others.

- When you receive feedback, you can learn how well your behavior matches your intentions.

- These skills are often not learned in dysfunctional families. Therefore, even though you put a lot of effort into managing your public image, you may not have a realistic view of how others perceive you. Receiving non-judgmental feedback is useful in learning to match your intentions with your actions.

2) The facilitator distributes **Guidelines for Giving and Receiving Feedback** and reviews the information in the handout.

3) The facilitator distributes **Feedback Yes, Interpretation No** and **Examples of Active Awareness and Feedback** and gives the following instructions:

➤ Make notes about a difficult situation you are involved in.

➤ Choose one that you are willing to discuss in this group.

☞ *Pause 5 minutes, then go on.*

➤ Now, I want each of you to talk about this situation for 3–5 minutes.

➤ While each person is talking, the others in the group should make notes for giving feedback observations to the speaker, using **Feedback Yes, Interpretation No.** Put each participant's name in the left column, and keep track of your observations of his or her facial expressions, body posture, gestures, voice volume and tone, verbal and non-verbal messages.

➤ Once each speaker has finished talking, the audience offers feedback observations to the speaker using the **Guidelines for Giving and Receiving Feedback, Examples of Active Awareness and Feedback** and **Feedback Yes, Interpretation No.**

➤ Using the **Guidelines for Giving and Receiving Feedback,** each speaker should also practice receiving feedback constructively.

➤ Finally, the facilitator gives feedback to the "feedback givers" about their methods. This helps participants fine-tune their skills.

➤ After each speaker finishes, the facilitator asks all the group members to evaluate how effectively they each gave or received feedback.

☞ *The entire process should take about 5–10 minutes per person.*

4) The facilitator leads a discussion with the following questions:

✔ How well do you think you followed the guidelines?

✔ Was it harder to give or to receive the feedback?

✔ What was the hardest guideline to follow?

✔ How is this different from the way you usually receive feedback?

✔ What have you learned from this exercise that you would like to remember and put into practice?

TRAINER'S NOTES

GUIDELINES FOR GIVING FEEDBACK

Non-judgmental feedback is a way of helping another person understand the effects of his or her behavior. Feedback helps people keep their behavior "on target" to better achieve their goals.

CRITERIA FOR USEFUL FEEDBACK

1. It is descriptive rather than evaluative.

2. It is specific rather than general.

3. It takes into account the needs of both the receiver and the giver of feedback.

4. It is directed toward behavior which the receiver can do something about.

5. It is solicited rather than imposed.

6. It is well-timed.

7. It is restated to make sure it is understood.

8. When feedback is given in a group, both giver and receiver have the opportunity to check with others in the group for accuracy of the feedback.

©1994 Whole Person Press 210 W Michigan Duluth MN 55802   (800) 247-6789

GUIDELINES TO RECEIVING FEEDBACK

1. Ask for it.

2. Accept it.

3. Do not make excuses.

4. Acknowledge its value.

5. Don't just sit there with a blank stare.

6. Express appreciation for it.

7. Discuss it. Don't just say, "Thank you," and let it drop.

8. View it as a continuing exploration.

9. Indicate what you intend to do with the feedback.

10. Don't become defensive.

11. Avoid getting mad, seeking revenge, or ignoring what is said or the person saying it.

12. Don't look for motives or hidden meanings.

13. Seek clarification.

14. Think about it and try to build on it.

©1994 Whole Person Press 210 W Michigan Duluth MN 55802   (800) 247-6789

EXAMPLES OF
ACTIVE AWARENESS AND FEEDBACK

Your eyes and ears are powerful tools for building relationships. Showing your awareness and checking to see if it is accurate is an important way to improve your understanding of others.

To practice active awareness and feedback, put what you observe into words.

1. Describe what you observe in the other person's face, especially in his or her eyes and mouth.
    "I am aware you're not looking at me."
    "I notice that you are smiling."
    "I see that your face looks flushed."

2. Describe what you observe in the other person's body posture and gestures, especially in his or her hands.
    "I am aware that you seem to be clenching your fists."
    "I notice that you keep shifting your position."

3. Describe what you observe in the other person's voice volume and voice tone.
    "I am aware that your voice seems very soft."

4. Point out observed differences between messages you are receiving.
    "You say you're relaxed, but your hands look tense to me."
    "You say you like me, but you don't seem to be looking at me."

5. Be sure to check out assumptions and interpretations; do not judge or label.
    "It looks like you are ___ . Are you?"
    "I believe that you are feeling ___ . How are you feeling?"
    "I am interpreting your behavior as ___ . How do you interpret it?"

6. When the other person's behavior affects you or your relationship, share your feelings to his or her behavior.
    "I notice that you are talking very loudly and I don't like that."
    "I am glad you decided to sit closer to me."

©1994 Whole Person Press 210 W Michigan Duluth MN 55802   (800) 247-6789

FEEDBACK YES, INTERPRETATION NO

Observations: Person	Face	Body posture	Gestures	Volume and tone of voice	Verbal and non-verbal messages
1					
2					
3					
4					
5					
6					
7					
8					
9					
10					

25 PLAY GROUP

Participants use recollections of childhood play to plan for more play in their adult lives.

GOALS

Recall and write down play activities from childhood.

Experience a childhood play activity.

Write a plan for including play in weekly activities.

GROUP SIZE

6–10

TIME FRAME

45–60 minutes

MATERIALS NEEDED

Paper, pencils, crayons, scissors; box of assorted children's toys.

> ☞ *Choose a variety of toys for the exercise (building blocks, toy cars and trucks, stuffed animals, and clay, etc.). The greater the variety, the more possibility for participants to choose familiar ways to express their playful qualities.*

PROCESS

1) The facilitator introduces the exercise by making the following points:

- People from dysfunctional families often take life and themselves very seriously.

- You may "struggle" to be better—a better manager, parent, friend, teacher, lover, etc. With such struggles there is little time for silliness or playfulness. The spontaneous childlike parts of you are ignored or lost.

- Children in a dysfunctional family are often deprived of the carefree play of childhood. Your time is spent taking care of a parent or sibling, mediating, or avoiding.

- As an adult you may expect yourself to work twice as hard as everyone else just to feel okay.

- It becomes increasingly important to have something to do *all* the time. Ultimately, you deny your need to play.

- The more you suffer, the more frightening it becomes to play in spontaneous or silly ways. Anything spontaneous has the potential of stirring up all the feelings and pain that are so carefully kept under wraps. Play may be viewed as a selfish, irresponsible, and useless activity.

2) The facilitator asks participants to make a list of the ways that they played when they were 4–6 years old. (5 minutes)

    ☞ *If you wish, give personal examples to help participants recall.*

3) The facilitator asks participants to walk around the room and talk about their lists with at least two other people. (5 minutes)

4) The facilitator places a box of children's toys in the middle of the room and gives these instructions:

    ➤ For the next 10 minutes, you are invited to play with anything in the box.

    ➤ You may play in the room in any way you wish. Create a game or a scenario, cooperate, play alone, whatever you like.

    ➤ Life is practice, and enjoying the process, acknowledging the present, is part of what brings joy to life.

    ➤ As a playful child, you can be in the present, enjoying this moment.

    ☞ *Participants may be uneasy and uncomfortable. They may giggle, withdraw, try to be in control, or get very silly. Many people from dysfunctional families learn to take life very seriously and not to be playful. During the exercise, if participants start commenting on the process and try to stop the exercise, encourage them to stay within the playful role. If some do withdraw from the exercise, encourage others to keep going for the full 10 minutes.*

5) After 10 minutes, the facilitator asks participants to stop the play activity and leads a discussion of the following questions:

    ✔ How did you feel during the play time?

    ✔ What is your most valuable childhood quality?

©1994 Whole Person Press 210 W Michigan Duluth MN 55802   (800) 247-6789

✔ How would your life be better if you expressed this quality more often?

✔ How could you increase or recapture this quality?

✔ What did your disapproving adult say to you to get you to stop playing?

6) The facilitator concludes with the following instructions:

➤ Write down a plan for playing with someone this week.

➤ Pick someone who you know can be playful.

➤ Be sure to tell the other person what you are trying to do and what you need from them, so that you can get the cooperation you need.

TRAINER'S NOTES

26 TRASH COMPACTOR

Participants identify angry feelings, learn some appropriate ways to express them, and make plans for dealing with anger in a new way.

GOALS

Identify specific people or events that are causing anger.

Recognize some methods for expressing anger appropriately.

Make plans for dealing with anger.

GROUP SIZE

6 or more

TIME FRAME

60–75 minutes

MATERIALS NEEDED

Newsprint, tape, and markers; copies of **Ways to Express Anger.**

PROCESS

1) The facilitator gives participants the following instructions:

> ➤ Take 3 large pieces of newsprint, some tape, and a marker.

> ➤ Tape the 3 papers to the wall, allowing plenty of space between you and the next person.

> ➤ Number the papers 1, 2, and 3.

> ➤ Standing at sheet 1, take 10 minutes to list 10 people or situations that you are mad about. These events could have happened today or 20 years ago.

>> ☞ *Having participants stand during this exercise makes them active, which helps them become aware of their true feelings. Some may want to write for more than 10 minutes. But letting them list every person or event that has made them angry is not the point of this exercise, so stop them at 10 minutes. Others may claim that they don't feel anger, so encourage them to write about*

    irritations, a low intensity form of anger. Sometimes this allows
    more intense feelings of anger to come out.

2) The facilitator gives the following instructions:

  ➤ Pick 1 person or situation you are mad about from sheet 1 and copy
    it to sheet 2.

  ➤ Write in large letters to fill the page.

3) The facilitator asks participants to sit down and gives a chalktalk,
   making the following points:

- We often keep a storehouse of anger inside. We can call this
  storehouse a "trash compactor." Here's how it works. Whenever you
  come across a feeling or thought you do not want to deal with
  directly, you put it in your personal trash compactor, hiding your
  thoughts and feelings from yourself and from others.

- If you get upset or irritated by someone, you may say "I don't want
  to hurt their feelings." Then you put this irritated feeling in your trash
  compactor, mash it down into your other unfinished business, and
  close the lid.

- When you hide what you believe are inappropriate feelings, they
  come out anyway. You may find yourself smiling while slamming
  kitchen cabinet doors.

- Real kitchen trash compactors get filled up eventually. The seams of
  the bag begin to split or the motor whines and moans when you try
  to crush more trash. Then it is time to take the trash out.

- Your personal trash compactor gets filled too, usually with anger.
  When your trash compactor is filled, you may have a tolerance
  break, and your usual calm and kind nature vanishes. You may
  become demanding, or start yelling at the person or about the event
  that made you angry.

- Very soon after, you may be embarrassed and apologetic about your
  outburst. The feelings that caused the outburst had little to do with
  what was going on at the moment. It just happened to be the last
  angry feeling that you tried to stuff in your trash compactor. During
  a tolerance break, the "nice lady" can become a raging woman. This
  is frightening to you and others. It usually knocks you for a loop.

- There are ways to express anger that will prevent this cycle of
  overstuffing your trash compactor and having a tolerance break.

©1994 Whole Person Press 210 W Michigan Duluth MN 55802   (800) 247-6789

4) The facilitator distributes the **Ways to Express Anger** worksheet and discusses the ideas giving personal examples.

5) The facilitator concludes with the following instructions:

➤ Read the **Ways to Express Anger** worksheet, then stand at sheet 3 and list 5 things that you will do during the next week to deal with your anger about the situation written on sheet 2. You have 5 minutes.

➤ Discuss your reactions with the group.

TRAINER'S NOTES

WAYS TO EXPRESS ANGER

FEEL THE EMOTION

Anger is emotional energy like any other emotion. It is just as valid as any other feeling. If it is there, feel it. When you get mad, you may need to move. You can feel the energy coursing through you, and it feels like it is going to bust out. Your heart beats harder and you breathe faster.

LOOK AT THE THINKING
THAT GOES WITH THE EMOTION

Consider the thoughts that go along with your anger. See if you recognize any patterns. To get free of the anger, try to change your thinking. You may think, *If I am late, everyone will think badly of me*, but you can change that thought to, *If I am late, the meeting will start late, but it won't make that much difference.*

MAKE A RESPONSIBLE DECISION
ABOUT WHAT ACTION, IF ANY, YOU WANT TO TAKE

Figure out what the anger is telling you. Do you have some unmet needs? Are there some things going on in your environment that you need to change? You may have to tell someone what you need. You can ask yourself, "Am I afraid of being left out? Am I afraid to do something by myself?" Sometimes you may get mad at a person who is late and did not call to tell you. If you get mad at this person, ask yourself what the anger is about. Are you afraid there has been a car accident, or insulted that your feelings weren't taken into consideration? Once you know what is behind these feelings, you can ask the person for what you need to cope with these feelings.

DON'T LET ANGER CONTROL YOU

Screaming may help. You do not need to continue to scream. Sometimes other things are needed as well. It is best if you decide that for yourself. You may need time out, so go to a peaceful place away from the object of your anger and think about what you want.

OPENLY AND HONESTLY DISCUSS YOUR ANGER
WHEN IT IS APPROPRIATE

Be aware of how you approach people and do not try to talk to a drunk, angry, hungry, or tired person. Pick the time and place so the other person will be most likely to listen. Picking your time can make a big difference in the presentation and the response.

MORE WAYS TO EXPRESS ANGER

TAKE RESPONSIBILITY FOR YOUR ANGER
You are angry. Someone did not *make* you angry. What they did may have been the catalyst, but you are responsible for your response. People often say, "He made me angry because he would not do what I told him." However, your emotional response is a result of your own interpretation and experience. No one can make you feel anything. When people say, "You made me do it, you made me lose control," they are saying, "I do not want to take responsibility for my own response and feelings."

BURN OFF THE ANGER ENERGY
Engage in some activity to use up the energy. Wash the car, jog, clean a closet, turn the music up loud and dance. If you physically discharge the energy, you can stop reacting and think more clearly about the situation.

DO NOT HIT WHEN FEELING ANGRY
Do not allow yourself to physically hit anyone or allow others to abuse you when you are angry. If abuse has occurred, seek professional help. Because the physical energy can be intense, hitting and throwing things is commonplace. Men are taught to express their feelings physically; most would never consider crying. However, striking another person in order to express anger is an unacceptable way to burn off energy.

WRITE LETTERS YOU DO NOT SEND
Write out your feelings to those with whom you are angry. You can discharge a lot of negative energy by writing down your resentments. This may help you to eliminate guilt and to become more clear about what you want from the other person. When you are clear about what you want you become less angry and out of control. You are able to communicate more clearly, be aware of your feelings, and not alienate the other person.

GET RID OF THE GUILT
Do not hold on to guilt. Throw it all away. It does not help to feel like a victim. Whenever you feel guilt, imagine that you put it in a shoe box, put the lid on the box, put the box in the closet, and close the door. Whenever you feel guilty later, imagine doing this again. Do not carry guilt around with you. Leave it behind.

©1994 Whole Person Press 210 W Michigan Duluth MN 55802   (800) 247-6789

27 ASSERTIVENESS

Participants learn different ways to express their needs, and practice appropriate assertiveness.

GOALS

Learn four common styles of expressing needs, desires, and opinions.

Understand the rights and responsibilities of effective communication of needs, desires, and opinions.

Practice skills in responsible assertive communication.

GROUP SIZE

Unlimited

TIME FRAME

60–90 minutes

MATERIALS NEEDED

Paper and pencils; copies of **Communication Styles, General Guidelines for Assertive Behavior, Assertive Rights, Assertive Responsibilities, Thinking Through an Assertive Response,** and **Evaluating Your Assertive Response.**

PROCESS

1) The facilitator distributes copies of **Assertive Rights** and **Assertive Responsibilities** to the participants, reviews the communication styles list, and gives examples of each.

2) The facilitator gives the following instructions:

   ➤ Think about a time when you wished you had done or said something different, something more assertive, a time when you had not stood up for yourself or said what you were thinking and feeling.

   ☞ *Give a personal example.*

   ➤ Now write about that time and what you wish you had said.

3) After 5 minutes, the facilitator distributes copies of **Thinking Through an Assertive Response** and tells participants to complete the worksheet.

4) After 5–8 minutes, the facilitator distributes and reviews the material in **General Guidelines for Assertive Behavior** and **Evaluating Your Assertive Response,** making these comments:

- Assertiveness is especially valued by Caucasian Americans, and the skills taught here are based on this assumption. What do other cultures that you have experienced think about assertiveness?

- Accept your current skill level, and practice to become more skilled.

- People have very different levels of ability in assertiveness. It is difficult for some, and almost too easy for others.

5) The facilitator asks participants to form groups of 3 and gives the following instructions:

➤ Each of you will take turns playing the roles of speaker, listener, and evaluator.

➤ One person plays the speaker and makes the assertive response written on the worksheet **Thinking Through an Assertive Response.**

➤ Another plays the listener, the recipient of the assertive response.

➤ And the third person evaluates the speaker's assertive response by using the **Evaluating An Assertive Response** worksheet.

➤ After you speak, use the **General Guidelines for Assertive Behavior** worksheet to evaluate your own performance.

➤ After the evaluation is done for each speaker, change roles until you each play the speaker, listener, and evaluator.

6) The facilitator reconvenes the group and concludes with the following questions:

✔ What role was hardest for you?

✔ Who is it hardest for you to be assertive with?

✔ What elements of assertiveness do you need to practice?

✔ Who can you practice with comfortably?

ASSERTIVE RIGHTS

1.   To have angry or illogical feelings.

2.   To be treated as a capable person and not to be patronized.

3.   To have my opinions be respected and considered.

4.   To make mistakes.

5.   To take the time needed to respond to requests.

6.   To make requests of others.

7.   To determine how to use my time.

8.   To say "no" to requests.

9.   To choose personal values.

10.   To have my needs be as important as those of others.

11.   To change my thinking and/or behavior.

12.   To strive for personal growth through whatever ethical channels are natural for my talents and interests.

13.   To share authentic relationships.

14.   To have idiosyncrasies.

ASSERTIVE RESPONSIBILITIES

1. To assess my true feelings without exaggeration or under-estimation; to express my feelings appropriately without demeaning someone else in the process.

2. To act in a responsible manner as much of the time as possible.

3. To think through my opinions and realize others can disagree with them.

4. To learn from mistakes, rather than punishing myself or others because of mistakes.

5. To reply as soon as possible, and without taking an unreasonable amount of time.

6. To accept others' answers respectfully; to carry out any commitments made.

7. To respect commitments to others as well as to myself; to allow sufficient time to fulfill commitments.

8. To think through my responses before answering.

9. To not impose my own values on others.

10. To express my needs and, if appropriate, work out a compromise.

11. To avoid "boxing in" myself or others by labeling or making judgments.

12. To acknowledge and appreciate each individual's choices and accomplishments; to enjoy the process.

13. To feel appropriate anger and joy, and to assert these feelings with the people involved.

14. To recognize anger and joy, and see that these feelings do not interfere with others' rights and responsibilities.

COMMUNICATION STYLES

Assertive: Behavior that enables a person to act in her own best interests, to stand up for herself without undue anxiety, to express wants and feelings directly with reasonable comfort, and to express personal rights without denying the rights of others.

Passive: Behavior that does not express an individual's rights, wants, and feelings directly. It is characterized by silence and no indication of feelings, and frequently results in conceding to the wants of others.

Passive-Aggressive: Behavior that does not express an individual's rights, wants, and feelings directly. The person seems to be passive, but there is a mixed message (i.e., rolling his eyes while saying he would be glad to help). Later, behavior emerges that expresses feelings of anger or hostility.

Aggressive: Behavior that expresses personal rights, wants, and feelings while infringing on the rights of others.

©1994 Whole Person Press 210 W Michigan Duluth MN 55802   (800) 247-6789

THINKING THROUGH
AN ASSERTIVE RESPONSE

A situation in which I would like to act assertively is:

In this situation, the rights I believe I have are:

In this situation, I feel the other person's rights are:

My feelings before asserting myself are:

Self-talk that is blocking me from acting assertively:

To challenge these irrational self-statements, I will tell myself:

What is important to me in this situation (What do I want to say or do?):

To respond assertively in this situation, I will say:

After responding assertively, I will probably feel:

GENERAL GUIDELINES
FOR ASSERTIVE BEHAVIOR

General questions you can ask yourself as you evaluate your own efforts toward increasing assertive behaviors.

WHAT DID I SAY?

1. Were my comments concise and to the point?
2. Was my statement appropriately assertive? Too aggressive? Too passive?
3. Was my statement definitive and firm?
4. Did I make a request for new behavior?

HOW DID I SAY IT?

1. Did I hesitate before saying what I wanted to say?
2. Did I stutter, stammer, lose my train of thought? Or was I fairly articulate?
3. Was my voice whining, pleading, or sarcastic?
4. Was I able to maintain eye contact?
5. Did I talk too loudly? Too softly?
6. Did my physical stance and gestures communicate assertiveness? Hostility? Passivity? Uneasiness?
7. Was my facial expression consistent with the verbal message I conveyed?

HOW DO I FEEL ABOUT HOW I SAID IT?

1. Was I pleased with my performance?
2. Did I feel uncomfortable, uptight, or upset afterwards?
3. Did I feel more assured afterwards?
4. Did I feel positive about myself?

EVALUATING AN ASSERTIVE RESPONSE

The following components should be part of assertive behavior. Use this checklist to make sure that your assertive response fulfills the following requirements:

_____ **Eye contact:** You looked directly at the person to whom you were speaking.

_____ **Body posture:** You faced the person, stood or sat comfortably close, leaned forward.

_____ **Gestures:** You used gestures to give added emphasis, but didn't overdo it.

_____ **Facial expression:** Your facial expression matched your message.

_____ **Content:** You accurately expressed how you felt and what you wanted to communicate.

_____ **Timing of response:** You responded spontaneously, but only after considering the appropriateness of the assertion and how the other person would receive it.

_____ **Ask for behavior change:** You asked for the change in behavior, but used good judgment. You were sensitive and understanding about the situation and the other person's rights.

28 MUSIC MEMORIES

Participants use music to evoke the feelings of a painful past relationship, and plan to change harmful behaviors associated with that relationship.

GOALS

Identify feelings connected with a painful past relationship.

Identify behaviors connected with this relationship.

Discuss how behaviors connected with the relationship were changed or should be changed.

GROUP SIZE

5–10

TIME FRAME

60–100 minutes

MATERIALS NEEDED

Audiocassette tape player and copies of **Music and My Relationships** worksheet.

> ☞ *This exercise is for ongoing groups that meet at least 3 times. Step 1 must be completed prior to the session in which you plan to use this exercise.*

PROCESS

1) The facilitator distributes copies of **Music and My Relationships** and gives the following instructions:

> ➤ I want you to bring a song or piece of music to the next session. It should be 3–5 minutes long and on audiocassette tape. The music should be connected to some painful relationship in your past that still brings back strong feelings.

> ➤ Listen to the song before the next session and fill out the **Music and My Relationships** worksheet.

> ➤ Bring the cassette and the completed **Music and My Relation-ships** worksheet to the next session.

©1994 Whole Person Press 210 W Michigan Duluth MN 55802   (800) 247-6789

2) At the next session, the facilitator gives these instructions:

➤ One at a time, volunteer to play your music.

➤ When someone's music is playing, please remain quiet and listen to the music. After you each play your music, you will talk about your answers to the questions from **Music and My Relationships.**

➤ When someone is talking about a relationship, resist the urge to interrupt. Listen to the story.

➤ Each of you will have time to play your music and discuss your specific relationship memories.

➤ End each discussion by talking about how you can change or have changed the behavior connected to this relationship.

3. After each person finishes, the facilitator asks participants to discuss their reactions to the feelings expressed by the music player.

TRAINER'S NOTES

©1994 Whole Person Press 210 W Michigan Duluth MN 55802   (800) 247-6789

MUSIC AND MY RELATIONSHIPS

What relationship do you associate with the music?

What feelings do you associate with the music?

What was your behavior like in this relationship?

What did you learn from this relationship? How have you done things differently since then? What changes should you continue to make?

29 SETTING NEW BOUNDARIES

An action-reflection exercise that helps participants recognize, respect, and apply their own boundaries.

GOALS

Identify personal boundaries and limits.

Establish new boundaries or limits to fit personal needs.

GROUP SIZE

Unlimited

TIME FRAME

60–90 minutes

MATERIALS NEEDED

Large sheets of newsprint, markers, and copies of the **New Boundaries** worksheet.

PROCESS

1) The facilitator makes the following points to introduce the exercise:

- You need to have boundaries between yourself and the outside world. This is necessary for you to be an individual with your own needs, ideas, opinions, and gifts. If your boundaries are too rigid, with no room for others to be near you emotionally, you can become isolated. If your boundaries are too permeable, you can become so flexible that you don't have independent actions or opinions.

- One goal in recovery is to develop boundaries that are neither too flexible nor too rigid. Developing healthy boundaries is your responsibility.

- You can't afford to give up the responsibility for taking care of yourself.

- As you develop healthy boundaries:

    - You develop an appropriate sense of the roles played by family members and by others.

- You learn to respect others and yourself.

- You don't use or abuse others or allow others to use or abuse you.

- You stop abusing yourself.

- You don't control others or let others control you.

- You stop taking responsibility for other people and stop letting them take responsibility for you.

- If you are rigid, you loosen up a bit.

- You develop a clearer sense of your rights and the rights of others.

- You learn to respect other people's territory as well as your own.

- You learn to listen to and trust yourself.

- You learn what hurts, what feels good, what is yours, and what isn't.

- You learn what you are willing to lose.

2) The facilitator distributes newsprint and markers to each participant and moves chairs aside, leaving space in the center.

3) The facilitator then gives the following instructions:

➤ Go to the center of the room and put your paper on the floor.

➤ Stand on your newsprint and use a marker to draw your boundary around yourself.

➤ Spend 3 minutes negotiating with others to find ways to make contact with each other physically while maintaining your own boundary.

➤ Now experiment with crossing your own boundary or another's boundary that is "mapped" on the floor.

4) The facilitator asks participants to remain standing and to answer the following questions.

✔ How did you feel after you drew your boundary?

✔ What feelings did you have when you made physical contact with others?

    ✔ How did you feel when you experimented and crossed your own or another's boundary?

    ✔ What did you feel when someone crossed your boundary?

5) The facilitator asks participants to sit down, distributes the **New Boundaries** worksheet, and asks participants to fill it out.

6) The facilitator presents the following points to conclude the exercise:

- When you identify the need to set a limit with someone, set it clearly, preferably without anger, and in as few words as possible.

- You cannot simultaneously set a boundary (a limit) and take care of another person's feelings.

- Anger, rage, complaining, and whining are clues that boundaries need to be set.

- Other people will test you when you set boundaries.

- Be prepared to follow through by acting in congruence with your boundaries.

- Some people are happy to respect your boundaries.

- You will set boundaries when you are ready, and not a minute sooner.

- A support system can be helpful as you strive to establish and enforce boundaries.

TRAINER'S NOTES

©1994 Whole Person Press 210 W Michigan Duluth MN 55802   (800) 247-6789

NEW BOUNDARIES

1. What is one boundary you have recently set?

2. Can you remember how you felt before and after you set the boundary?

3. Were you called on to enforce it?

4. What are the most difficult kinds of boundaries for you to set and enforce?

5. Is somebody in your life using you, or not treating you appropriately or respectfully now?

6. Are you angry, whining, constantly complaining or upset about something?

7. What is preventing you from taking care of yourself?

8. What do you think will happen if you do?

9. What do you think will happen if you don't?

10. How do you feel when you are around people with rigid boundaries (too many rules and regulations)?

11. How do you feel when you are around people with few, or no boundaries (they will do anything you suggest or agree with all that you say)?

12. In the past, what have you been willing to lose for the sake of a particular relationship?

13. What are you willing to lose now?

14. What are you not willing to lose?

Resources

RESOURCE LIST

The resources listed here have been used in developing this book, and are useful for leaders working with people from dysfunctional families. Reading about recovery from different viewpoints is helpful for finding an approach to your own work with groups. These resources offer a variety of ways to encourage recovery and healing. They provide background information and help you improve your counseling skills. Group participants will also find them beneficial for progressing further in their recovery work.

A word of caution. Some recovering people read many books and learn to "talk the talk" without learning to "walk the walk." They may be unable to live what they learn. Reading recovery books can become one more obsessive activity. At some point, you need to encourage participants to stop reading and concentrate on making behavioral changes in their lives.

Bass, Ellen, and Laura Davis. *The Courage to Heal: A Guide for Women Survivors of Child Sexual Abuse*. New York: Harper and Row, 1988.

This inspiring, comprehensive guide offers hope and encouragement to any woman or man who was sexually abused as a child and to those who care about her or him. The authors weave together personal experience and professional knowledge to show the reader how to come to terms with the past while moving powerfully into the future. There are clear explanations, practical suggestions, a map of the healing journey, and moving examples of the recovery process.

Beattie, Melody. *Codependent No More: How to Stop Controlling Others and Start Caring for Yourself*. New York: Harper and Row, 1987.

The author, a recovering alcoholic and former chemical dependency counselor, details the characteristics of codependency, where the behavior comes from and how it affects us and those around us. She offers hope and guidance, discusses several options to control behavior, and helps you understand that letting go will set you free.

Beattie, Melody. *Beyond Codependency and Getting Better All the Time*. San Francisco: Harper and Row, 1989.

The author's second book moves beyond understanding codependency to exploring the dynamics of recovery, the role recycling plays as a normal—

even necessary—part of recovery and how positive affirmations can counter negative messages. This book is for those who want to survive and are ready to grow in the realization that recovery from codependency is a life-long process.

Black, Claudia. *Repeat After Me*. Denver: M.A.C. Printing and Publications, 1981.

Troubled families produce troubled children who grow into adults with problems. This is a self-help book designed to provide the reader with a step-by-step method for overcoming those problems and beginning a healthier, happier lifestyle. The author walks the reader through the problems, then gives the reader a series of exercises and suggestions to let the wellness process begin.

Black, Claudia. *Double Duty: Dual Dynamics Within the Chemically Dependent Home*. New York: Ballantine Books, 1990.

Adult children of alcoholics may have had a second dynamic in their dysfunctional homes. They may have had to deal with two chemically dependent parents or physical or sexual abuse. They may be people of color, only children, gay or lesbian, physically disabled, or themselves chemically dependent or food addicted. Using life stories with illuminating commentary, the author provides hope for recovery.

Bradshaw, John. *Homecoming: Reclaiming and Championing Your Inner Child*. New York: Bantam Books, 1990.

To help people champion their inner child, the author offers a wealth of practical techniques: giving your child permission to break destructive family rules and roles; teaching new rules that allow pleasure and honest self-expression; learning to deal with anger and difficult relationships; paying attention to our innermost purpose and desires. He shows how the reclaimed child can become a "wonder child," the source of new energy for living.

Cermak, Timmen L. *Diagnosing and Treating Co-dependence: A Guide for Professionals Who Work with Chemical Dependents, Their Spouses and Children*. Minneapolis: Johnson Institute Books, 1986.

Dr. Cermak presents clear diagnostic criteria for co-dependency and illustrates them with examples. He speaks to all helping professionals about ways of treating co-dependence.

Co-dependency: An Emerging Issue. Hollywood, FL: Health Communications, Inc., 1985.

Several authors contributed articles for this book, which covers many issues related to alcoholism. There are chapters on sexuality, addiction to the addict, personality disturbances, intimacy, and the warning signs of alcoholism.

Davis, Laura. *The Courage to Heal Workbook: For Women and Men Survivors of Child Sexual Abuse*. New York: Harper and Row, 1990.

In this groundbreaking companion volume to *The Courage to Heal*, the author has created an innovative, inspiring, and in-depth workbook that speaks to all women and men healing from the effects of child sexual abuse. With its combination of checklists, open-ended questions, writing exercises, art projects, and activities, the book takes the survivor step-by-step through key aspects of the healing process.

Friel, John, and Linda Friel. *Adult Children: The Secrets of Dysfunctional Families*. Deerfield Beach, FL: Health Communications, Inc., 1988.

The authors explore experiences from growing up in a dysfunctional family that was characterized by perfectionism, workaholism, compulsive overeating, intimacy problems, depression, and problems in expressing feelings. The authors provide a readable explanation of what happens in this type of family and give suggestions for change.

Halpern, Howard M. *Cutting Loose: An Adult Guide to Coming to Terms with Your Parents*. Toronto: Bantam Books, 1983

The author describes how people get stuck in frustrating parent/child patterns and how to get out of them. He talks about the tactics of the Martyred Mom, the Despotic Dad, moralistic parents, seductive parents, aging parents, and more. He shows you how you can break the old routines and begin to have a better, happier relationship with your parents, as equals, even as friends.

Hay, Louise L. *You Can Heal Your Life*. Santa Monica, CA: Hay House, 1984.

The author, a metaphysical counselor and workshop leader who was once diagnosed with terminal cancer, says that "if you are willing to do the mental work, almost anything can be healed." She offers practical steps for dissolving both the fears and causations of diseases. She devotes her life to assisting others in discovering and using the full potential of their own creative powers.

Hendricks, Gay, and Kathlyn Hendricks. *Conscious Loving: The Journey to Co-Commitment*. New York: Bantam Books, 1990.

An exciting book that explores the precise cause of co-dependency and how you can break free of this painful distortion of love. Readers learn about co-commitment, a way to be together without giving up your self. The second part of the book provides 34 exercises to heal old hurts, build real communication and trust, find lost feelings, and deepen your capacity for pleasure, security, and intimacy.

Hetherington, Cheryl. *Bringing Your Self to Life: Changing Co-Dependent Patterns*, Iowa City: Rudi Publishing, 1989.

A warmly illustrated, easy-to-read book that offers stories about people in your life—families, friends, co-workers. Co-dependency is defined in terms that everyone can understand. With special sections on women and helping professionals, it is a practical guide with activities to help people take better care of themselves and learn to change patterns.

Houston, Jean. *The Possible Human: A Course in Enhancing Your Physical, Mental, and Creative Abilities*. New York: J.P. Tarcher, Inc., 1982.

This is a book version of the author's mind-expansion workshops. The exercises are designed to show you how you can see more, hear more, remember more, and draw on more of your inner resources. It teaches you how to gain access to hidden images, ideas, and sensory-based memories, employing strategies used successfully by writers, artists, teachers, therapists, actors, athletes, scientists, and business executives.

Howe, Gerry. *Listen to the Heart: The Transformational Pathway to Health and Wellness*. Iowa City: Rudi Publishing, 1991.

The author offers a refreshing approach to wellness—his own path to help the reader learn new skills and perspectives that assist in making choices to live more fully.

Kubler-Ross, Elisabeth. *Death and Dying*. New York: Collier, 1969.

The author, a medical doctor, psychiatrist, and internationally renowned thanatologist, brought death out of the darkness. She has helped thousands of people deal with personal losses by helping them understand the grieving process as healthy and natural. She offers hope for the understanding of human strengths and weaknesses experienced during a difficult time.

Lerner, Harriet Goldhor. *Dance of Anger: A Woman's Guide to Changing the Patterns of Intimate Relationships*. New York: Harper and Row, 1985.

This book provides a helpful guide to understanding and reducing anger in close relationships by showing how anger works to maintain the status quo as well as to change it. Dr. Lerner, a psychotherapist at the Menninger Foundation, gives readers information they can use to manage anger wisely and well.

Lerner, Harriet Goldhor. *Dance of Intimacy: A Woman's Guide to Courageous Acts of Change in Key Relationships*. New York: Harper and Row, 1989.

The author takes a careful look at those relationships where intimacy is most challenged by too much distance, too much intensity, or simply too much pain. She illustrates how you can move differently in these key relationships.

Maxwell, Ruth. *The Booze Battle*. New York: Ballantine Books, 1980.

This book is written for the spouse, partner, boss, or friend of the alcoholic. It is helpful for learning what to do to take better care of your own needs and to recover from enabling or codependent patterns. The techniques can lead you to seek help, get more control of your life, be less blaming and angry, and get happier.

Peele, Stanton. *Love and Addiction*. New York: Signet, 1975.

This is one of the earliest books about the addictive nature of relationships. The author, a social psychologist, describes how we turn to one another or alcohol and other drugs to meet needs. He explains that addiction is really psychological, social, and cultural, and he presents clear guidelines for analyzing existing relationships in terms of their potential for mutual growth.

Robinson, Bryan E. *Work Addiction*. Deerfield Beach, FL: Health Communications, Inc., 1989.

Robinson says that work addiction is the most acceptable yet dangerous form of addiction. He shows us how and why adult children from dysfunctional families become super-responsible and compulsive workers, and how work addiction can destroy the family just like any other addiction. He distinguishes between healthy work production and compulsive overworking, lets readers test themselves for addictive tendencies, and provides a plan for recovery.

Rubin, Lillian. *Intimate Strangers: Men and Women Together*. New York: Harper and Row, 1982.

The author writes the book for every woman and man who yearns for an intimate relationship with the other sex and wonders why it seems so elusive. She explains how the differences between men and women affect such critical issues as intimacy, sexuality, dependency, work, and parenting. She writes of the "approach-avoidance dance" of intimacy, "redefining dependency," and the "sexual dilemma."

Satir, Virginia. *Peoplemaking*. Palo Alto, CA: Science and Behavior Books, Inc., 1972.

An expert in family therapy, the author writes this engaging and interesting book about becoming a more nurturing parent. It is appropriate for the average family and provides a process for reviewing family patterns and guidelines for remapping a more nurturing family style. The book is a workbook with exercises that families can use to learn new levels of family communication.

Schaef, Anne Wilson. *Escape From Intimacy*. San Francisco: Harper and Row, 1989.

The author examines the problem of addictions to sex, romance, and relationships, clearly defining where healthy activities end and addictive behaviors begin. This book is for those struggling to overcome "love" addictions—disorders that can destroy relationships and careers.

Sher, Barbara. *Wishcraft: How to Get What You Really Want*. New York: Ballantine Books, 1979.

The author offers effective strategies for making real change in your life. This human, practical program puts your vague yearnings and dreams to work—with concrete results. The book helps readers to discover strengths and skills, turn fears and negative feelings into positive tools, diagram the path to goals, and map out target dates for meeting them.

Siegel, Bernie. *Peace, Love and Healing*. New York: Harper and Row, 1989.

The emphasis of this book is on self-healing, the ability given to us by a creator and one ignored by medicine. Modern medicine and self-healing can be cooperative. The book challenges us, whether we are well or ill, to recognize how our mind influences our body and how to use this knowledge to our advantage.

©1994 Whole Person Press 210 W Michigan Duluth MN 55802   (800) 247-6789

Wegscheider, Sharon. *Another Chance: Hope and Health for the Alcoholic Family*. Palo Alto, CA: Science and Behavior Books, Inc., 1981.

This is a helpful guide for physicians, counselors, lawyers, ministers, and other helping professionals who must deal with the difficult problems of alcoholics and their families. Its easy to read style and moving human stories also invite the lay person to share its message of hope. For the millions of Americans who suffer under the burden of their own or a loved one's alcoholism, it offers fresh insights on what is happening in their families and what they personally can do to change it.

Wegscheider-Cruse, Sharon. *Coupleship: How to Build a Relationship*. Deerfield Beach, FL: Health Communications, Inc., 1985.

Forming a happy, joy-filled partnership is one of the greater challenges in life. In this book you will find ideas and tools to enhance a current marriage or partnership, make a decision about commitment, explore ways to find a partner, and learn about "romance responsibility," "romance invaders," "sexuality," "intimacy," and much more.

Woititz, Janet Geringer. *Adult Children of Alcoholics*. Pompano Beach, FL: Health Communications, Inc., 1983.

Although originally written only with children of alcoholics in mind, the material in this book applies to other types of dysfunctional families as well. If you did not grow up with alcoholism, but lived with other compulsive behaviors such as gambling, drug abuse, or overeating, or if you experienced chronic illness, profound religious attitudes, or were adopted, lived in foster care, or in other potentially dysfunctional systems, you may find that you identify with the characteristics presented in the book.

Woititz, Janet Geringer. *Struggle for Intimacy*. Pompano Beach, FL: Health Communications, Inc., 1985.

A human relations counselor, the author writes about the struggles that adult children of alcoholics have with intimate relationships. She defines a healthy relationship and discusses the difficulties that children of alcoholics have in finding and keeping healthy relationships. Some of these include fear of abandonment and loss of self, anger, guilt, shame, and depression.

WHOLE PERSON ASSOCIATES RESOURCES

Our materials are designed to address the whole person—physical, emotional, mental, spiritual, and social. Developed for trainers by trainers, all of these resources are ready-to-use. Novice trainers will find everything they need to get started, and the expert trainer will discover new ideas and concepts to add to their existing programs.

GROUP PROCESS RESOURCES

All of the exercises in our group process resources encourage interaction between the leader and participants, as well as among the participants. Each exercise includes everything you need to present a meaningful program: goals, optimal group size, time frame, materials list, and the complete process instructions.

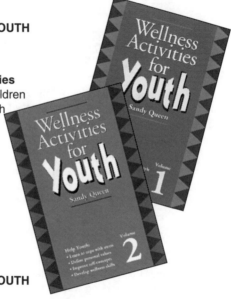

WELLNESS ACTIVITIES FOR YOUTH
Volumes 1 & 2
Sandy Queen

Each volume of **Wellness Activities for Youth** helps leaders teach children and teenagers about wellness with a whole person approach, a "no put-down" rule, and most of all, an emphasis on FUN. The concepts include:

- values
- stress and coping
- self-esteem
- personal well-being
- social wellness

WELLNESS ACTIVITIES FOR YOUTH WORKSHEET MASTERS

Complete packages of full-size (8 1/2" x 11") photocopy masters that include all the worksheets and handouts from **Wellness Activities for Youth Volumes 1 and 2** are available to you. Use the masters for easy duplication of the handouts for each participant.

- ❑ **WY1 / Wellness Activities for Youth Volume 1 / $19.95**
- ❑ **WY2 / Wellness Activities for Youth Volume 2 / $19.95**
- ❑ **WY1W / Wellness Activities for Youth V. 1 Worksheet Masters / $9.95**
- ❑ **WY2W / Wellness Activities for Youth V. 2 Worksheet Masters / $9.95**

WORKING WITH WOMEN'S GROUPS
Volumes 1 & 2
Louise Yolton Eberhardt

The two volumes of **Working with Women's Groups** have been completely revised and updated. These exercises will help women explore issues that are of perennial concern as well as today's hot topics.

Volume 1:
- consciousness-raising
- self-discovery
- assertiveness training

Volume 2:
- sexuality issues
- women of color
- leadership skills training

WORKING WITH WOMEN'S GROUPS
WORKSHEET MASTERS

Complete packages of full-size (8 1/2" x 11") photocopy masters that include all the worksheets and handouts from **Working with Women's Groups volume 1 and 2** are available to you. Use the masters for easy duplication of the handouts for each participant.

- ❏ **WG1 / Working with Women's Groups—Volume 1 / $24.95**
- ❏ **WG2 / Working with Women's Groups—Volume 2 / $24.95**
- ❏ **WG1W / Working with Women's Groups—Volume 1 Worksheet Masters / $9.95**
- ❏ **WG2W / Working with Women's Groups—Volume 2 Worksheet Masters / $9.95**

WORKING WITH MEN'S GROUPS
Roger Karsk and Bill Thomas

Also revised and updated, this volume is a valuable resource for anyone working with men's groups. The exercises cover a variety of topics, including:

- self discovery
- parenting
- conflict
- intimacy

- ❏ **MG / Working with Men's Groups / $24.95**
- ❏ **MGW / Working with Men's Groups Worksheet Masters / $9.95**

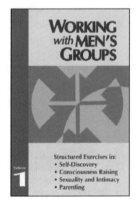

WORKING WITH GROUPS FROM DYSFUNCTIONAL FAMILIES

Cheryl Hetherington

This collection of 29 proven group activities is designed to heal the pain that results from growing up in or living in a dysfunctional family. With these exercises you can:

- promote healing
- build self-esteem
- encourage sharing
- help participants acknowledge their feelings

WORKING WITH GROUPS FROM DYSFUNCTIONAL FAMILIES REPRODUCIBLE WORKSHEET MASTERS

A complete package of full-size (8 1/2" x 11") photocopy masters that include all the worksheets and handouts from **Working with Groups from Dysfunctional Families** is available to you. Use the masters for easy duplication of the handouts for each participant.

- ❑ **DFH / Working with Groups from Dysfunctional Families / $24.95**
- ❑ **DFW / Dysfunctional Families Worksheet Masters / $9.95**

PLAYFUL ACTIVITIES FOR POWERFUL PRESENTATIONS

Bruce Williamson

This book contains 40 fun exercises designed to fit any group or topic. These exercises will help you:

- build teamwork
- encourage laughter and playfulness
- relieve stress and tension
- free up the imaginations of participants

- ❑ **PAP / Playful Activities for Powerful Presentations $19.95**

©1994 Whole Person Press 210 W Michigan Duluth MN 55802   (800) 247-6789

STRUCTURED EXERCISES
IN STRESS MANAGEMENT—VOLUMES 1-4
Nancy Loving Tubesing, EdD and Donald A. Tubesing, PhD, Editors

Each book in this four-volume series contains 36 ready-to-use teaching modules that involve the participant—as a whole person—in learning how to manage stress more effectively.

Each exercise is carefully designed by top stress-management professionals. Instructions are clearly written and field-tested so that even beginning trainers can smoothly lead a group through warm-up and closure, reflection and planning, and action and interaction—all with minimum preparation time.

Each Stress Handbook is brimming with practical ideas that you can weave into your own teaching designs or mix and match to develop new programs for varied settings, audiences, and time frames. In each volume you'll find **Icebreakers, Stress Assessments, Management Strategies, Skill Builders, Action Planners, Closing Processes** and **Group Energizers**—all with a special focus on stress management.

STRUCTURED EXERCISES
IN WELLNESS PROMOTION—VOLUMES 1-4
Nancy Loving Tubesing, EdD and Donald A. Tubesing, PhD, Editors

Discover the Wellness Handbooks—from the wellness pioneers at Whole Person Associates. Each volume in this innovative series includes 36 experiential learning activities that focus on whole person health—body, mind, spirit, emotions, relationships, and lifestyle.

The exercises, developed by an interdisciplinary pool of leaders in the wellness movement nationwide, actively encourage people to adopt wellness-oriented attitudes and to develop more responsible self-care patterns.

All process designs in the Wellness Handbooks are clearly explained and have been thoroughly field-tested with diverse audiences so that trainers can use them with confidence. **Icebreakers, Wellness Explorations, Self-Care Strategies, Action Planners, Closings** and **Group Energizers** are all ready-to-go—including reproducible worksheets, scripts, and chalktalk outlines—for the busy professional who wants to develop unique wellness programs without spending oodles of time in preparation.

©1994 Whole Person Press 210 W Michigan Duluth MN 55802   (800) 247-6789

STRUCTURED EXERCISES IN STRESS AND WELLNESS ARE AVAILABLE IN TWO FORMATS

LOOSE-LEAF FORMAT (8 1/2" x 11")

The loose-leaf, 3-ring binder format provides you with maximum flexiblity. The binder gives you plenty of room to add your own adaptations, workshop outlines, or notes right where you need them. The index tabs offer quick and easy access to each section of exercises, and the generous margins allow plenty of room for notes. In addition an extra set of the full-size worksheets and handouts are packaged separately for convenient duplication.

SOFTCOVER FORMAT (6" x 9")

The softcover format is a perfect companion to the loose-leaf version. This smaller book fits easily into your briefcase or bag, and the binding has been designed to remain open on your desk or lectern. Worksheets and handouts can be enlarged and photocopied for distribution to your participants, or you can purchase sets of worksheet masters.

WORKSHEET MASTERS

The Worksheet Masters for the two Structured Exercise series offer full-size (8 1/2" x 11") photocopy masters. All of the worksheets and handouts for each volume are reproduced in easy-to-read print with professional graphics. All you need to do to complete your workshop preparation is run them through a copier.

Structured Exercises in Stress Management

       ❏ **Loose-Leaf Edition—Volume 1-4 / $54.95 each**
       ❏ **Softcover Edition—Volume 1-4 / $29.95 each**
       ❏ **Worksheet Masters—Volume 1-4 / $9.95 each**

Structured Exercises in Wellness Promotion

       ❏ **Loose-Leaf Edition—Volume 1-4 / $54.95 each**
       ❏ **Softcover Edition—Volume 1-4 / $29.95 each**
       ❏ **Worksheet Masters—Volume 1-4 / $9.95 each**

©1994 Whole Person Press 210 W Michigan Duluth MN 55802   (800) 247-6789

WORKSHOPS-IN-A-BOOK

KICKING YOUR STRESS HABITS:
A Do-it-yourself Guide to Coping with Stress
Donald A. Tubesing, PhD

Over a quarter of a million people have found ways to deal with their everyday stress by using **Kicking Your Stress Habits**. This workshop-in-a-book actively involves the reader in assessing stressful patterns and developing more effective coping strategies with helpful "Stop and Reflect" sections in each chapter.

The 10-step planning process and 20 skills for managing stress make **Kicking Your Stress Habits** an ideal text for stress management classes in many different settings, from hospitals to universities and for a wide variety of groups.

❑ K / Kicking Your Stress Habits / 14.95

SEEKING YOUR HEALTHY BALANCE:
A Do-it-yourself Guide to Whole Person Well-being
Donald A. Tubesing, PhD and Nancy Loving Tubesing, EdD

Where can you find the time and energy to "do it all" without sacrificing your health and well-being? **Seeking Your Healthy Balance** helps the reader discover how to make changes toward a more balanced lifestyle by learning effective ways to juggle work, self, and others; clarifying self-care options; and discovering and setting their own personal priorities.

Seeking Your Healthy Balance asks the questions and helps readers find their own answers.

❑ HB / Seeking Your Healthy Balance / 14.95

©1994 Whole Person Press 210 W Michigan Duluth MN 55802   (800) 247-6789

RELAXATION RESOURCES

Many trainers and workshop leaders have discovered the benefits of relaxation and visualization in healing the body, mind, and spirit.

30 SCRIPTS FOR RELAXATION, IMAGERY, AND INNER HEALING
Julie Lusk

These two volumes are collections of relaxation scripts created by trainers for trainers. The 30 scripts in each of the two volumes have been professionally-tested and fine-tuned so they are ready to use for both novice and expert trainers.

Help your participants change their behavior, enhance their self-esteem, discover inner, private places, and heal themselves through simple trainer-led guided imagery scripts. Both volumes include information on how to use the scripts, suggestions for tailoring them to your specific needs and audience, and information on how to successfully incorporate guided imagery into your existing programs.

❑ **30S / 30 Scripts for Relaxation, Imagery, and Inner Healing—Volume 1 / $19.95**
❑ **30S2 / 30 Scripts for Relaxation, Imagery, and Inner Healing—Volume 2 / $19.95**

INQUIRE WITHIN
Andrew Schwartz

Use visualization to make positive changes in your life. The 24 visualization experiences in **Inquire Within** will help participants enhance their creativity, heal inner pain, learn to relax, and deal with conflict. Each visualization includes questions at the end of the process that encourage deeper reflection and a better understanding of the exercise and the response it invokes.

❑ **IW / Inquire Within / $19.95**

RELAXATION AUDIOTAPES

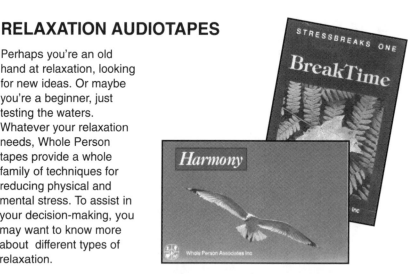

Perhaps you're an old hand at relaxation, looking for new ideas. Or maybe you're a beginner, just testing the waters. Whatever your relaxation needs, Whole Person tapes provide a whole family of techniques for reducing physical and mental stress. To assist in your decision-making, you may want to know more about different types of relaxation.

We offer six different types of relaxation techniques in our twenty-one tapes. The Whole Person series ranges from simple breathing and stretching exercises, to classic autogenic and progressive relaxation sequences, to guided meditations and whimsical daydreams. All are carefully crafted to promote whole person relaxation—body, mind, and spirit. We also provide a line of music-only tapes, composed specifically for relaxation.

SENSATIONAL RELAXATION

When stress piles up, it becomes a heavy load both physically and emotionally. These full-length relaxation experiences will teach you techniques that can be used whenever you feel that stress is getting out of control. Choose one you like and repeat it daily until it becomes second nature then recall that technique whenever you need it.

❑ **CD / Countdown to Relaxation / $9.95**
❑ **DS / Daybreak / Sundown / $9.95**
❑ **TDB / Take a Deep Breath / $9.95**
❑ **RLX / Relax . . . Let Go . . . Relax / $9.95**
❑ **SRL / StressRelease / $9.95**
❑ **WRM / Warm and Heavy / $9.95**

STRESS BREAKS

Do you need a short energy booster or a quick stress reliever? If you don't know what type of relaxation you like, or if you are new to guided relaxation techniques, try one of our Stress Breaks for a quick refocusing or change of pace any time of the day.

❑ **BT / BreakTime / $9.95**
❑ **NT / Natural Tranquilizers / $9.95**

DAYDREAMS

Escape from the stress around you with guided tours to beautiful places. Picture yourself traveling to the ocean, sitting in a park, luxuriating in the view from the majestic mountains, or enjoying the solitude and serenity of a cozy cabin. The 10-minute escapes included in our Daydream tapes will lead your imagination away from your everyday cares so you can resume your tasks relaxed and comforted.

    ❑ **DD1 / Daydreams 1: Getaways / $9.95**
    ❑ **DD2 / Daydreams 2: Peaceful Places / $9.95**

GUIDED MEDITATION

Take a step beyond relaxation and discover the connection between body and mind with guided meditation. The imagery in our full-length meditations will help you discover your strengths, find healing, make positive life changes, and recognize your inner wisdom.

    ❑ **IH / Inner Healing / $9.95**
    ❑ **PE / Personal Empowering / $9.95**
    ❑ **HBT / Healthy Balancing / $9.95**
    ❑ **SPC / Spiritual Centering / $9.95**

WILDERNESS DAYDREAMS

Discover the healing power of nature with the four tapes in the Wilderness Daydreams series. The eight special journeys will transport you from your harried, stressful surroundings to the peaceful serenity of words and water.

    ❑ **WD1 / Canoe / Rain / $9.95**
    ❑ **WD2 / Island /Spring / $9.95**
    ❑ **WD3 / Campfire / Stream / $9.95**
    ❑ **WD4 / Sailboat / Pond / $9.95**

MUSIC ONLY

No relaxation program would be complete without relaxing melodies that can be played as background to a prepared script or that can be enjoyed as you practice a technique you have already learned. Steven Eckels composed his melodies specifically for relaxation. These "musical prayers for healing" will calm your body, mind, and spirit.

    ❑ **T / Tranquility / $9.95**
    ❑ **H / Harmony / $9.95**
    ❑ **S / Serenity / $9.95**

Titles can be combined for discounts!

QUANTITY DISCOUNT			
1 - 9	10 - 49	50 - 99	100+
$9.95	$8.95	$7.96	CALL

©1994 Whole Person Press 210 W Michigan Duluth MN 55802   (800) 247-6789

ORDER FORM

Name _____

Address _____

City _____

State/Zip _____

Area Code/Telephone _____

Please make checks payable to:
Whole Person Associates Inc
210 West Michigan
Duluth MN 55802-1908
FAX: 1-218-727-0505
TOLL FREE: 1-800-247-6789

Books / Workshops-In-A-Book

___ Kicking Your Stress Habits .... $14.95 _____

___ Seeking Your Healthy Balance .... $14.95 _____

Structured Exercises in Stress Management Series—Volumes 1-4

___ Stress Softcover Edition .... Vol 1 ___ Vol 2 ___ Vol 3 ___ Vol 4 ___ $29.95 _____

___ Stress Loose-Leaf Edition .... Vol 1 ___ Vol 2 ___ Vol 3 ___ Vol 4 ___ $54.95 _____

___ Stress Worksheet Masters .... Vol 1 ___ Vol 2 ___ Vol 3 ___ Vol 4 ___ $9.95 _____

Structured Exercises in Wellness Promotion Series—Volumes 1-4

___ Wellness Softcover Edition .... Vol 1 ___ Vol 2 ___ Vol 3 ___ Vol 4 ___ $29.95 _____

___ Wellness Loose-Leaf Edition .... Vol 1 ___ Vol 2 ___ Vol 3 ___ Vol 4 ___ $54.95 _____

___ Wellness Worksheet Masters .... Vol 1 ___ Vol 2 ___ Vol 3 ___ Vol 4 ___ $9.95 _____

Group Process Resources

___ Playful Activities for Powerful Presentations .... $19.95 _____

___ Working with Groups from Dysfunctional Families .... $24.95 _____

___ Working with Groups from Dysfunctional Families Worksheet Masters .... $9.95 _____

___ Working with Women's Groups .... Vol 1 ___ Vol 2 ___ $24.95 _____

___ Working with Women's Groups Worksheet Masters .... Vol 1 ___ Vol 2 ___ $9.95 _____

___ Working with Men's Groups .... $24.95 _____

___ Working with Men's Groups Worksheet Masters .... $9.95 _____

___ Wellness Activities for Youth .... Vol 1 ___ Vol 2 ___ $19.95 _____

___ Wellness Activities for Youth Worksheet Masters .... Vol 1 ___ Vol 2 ___ $9.95 _____

Relaxation Audiotapes

___ BreakTime .... $ 9.95 _____

___ Countdown to Relaxation .... $ 9.95 _____

___ Daybreak/Sundown .... $ 9.95 _____

___ Daydreams 1: Getaways .... $ 9.95 _____

___ Daydreams 2: Peaceful Places .... $ 9.95 _____

___ Harmony (music only) .... $ 9.95 _____

___ Healthy Balancing .... $ 9.95 _____

___ Inner Healing .... $ 9.95 _____

___ Natural Tranquilizers .... $ 9.95 _____

___ Personal Empowering .... $ 9.95 _____

___ Relax . . . Let Go . . . Relax .... $ 9.95 _____

___ Serenity (music only) .... $ 9.95 _____

___ Spiritual Centering .... $ 9.95 _____

___ StressRelease .... $ 9.95 _____

___ Take a Deep Breath .... $ 9.95 _____

___ Tranquility (music only) .... $ 9.95 _____

___ Warm and Heavy .... $ 9.95 _____

___ Wilderness DD 1: Canoe/Rain .... $ 9.95 _____

___ Wilderness DD 2: Island/Spring .... $ 9.95 _____

___ Wilderness DD 3: Campfire/Stream .... $ 9.95 _____

___ Wilderness DD 4: Sailboat/Pond .... $ 9.95 _____

Relaxation Resources

___ 30 Scripts—Volume 1 .... $19.95 _____

___ 30 Scripts—Volume 2 .... $19.95 _____

___ Inquire Within .... $19.95 _____

My check is enclosed. **(US funds only)**

Please charge my_____Visa _____Mastercard

_____

Exp date _____

Signature _____

SUBTOTAL _____

TAX (MN residents 6.5%) _____

7% GST-Canadian customers only _____

***SHIPPING** _____

GRAND TOTAL _____

800-247-6789

** **SHIPPING**. $5.00 ($8.00 outside U.S.)
Please call us for quotes on UPS 3rd Day,
2nd Day or Next Day Air.

About Whole Person Associates

At Whole Person Associates, we're 100% committed to providing stress and wellness materials that involve participants and have a "whole person" focus—body, mind, spirit, and relationships.

That's our mission and it's very important to us—but it doesn't tell the whole story. Behind the products in our catalog is a company full of people—and *that's* what really makes us who we are.

ABOUT THE OWNERS

Whole Person Associates was created by the vision of two people: Donald A. Tubesing, PhD, and Nancy Loving Tubesing, EdD. Since way back in 1970, Don and Nancy have been active in the stress management/wellness promotion movement—consulting, leading seminars, writing, and publishing. Most of our early products were the result of their creativity and expertise.

Living proof that you can "stay evergreen," Don and Nancy remain the driving force behind the company and are still very active in developing new products that touch people's lives.

ABOUT THE COMPANY

Whole Person Associates was "born" in Duluth, Minnesota, and we remain committed to our lovely city on the shore of Lake Superior. All of our operations are here, which makes communication between departments much easier! We've grown since our beginnings, but at a steady pace—we're interested in sustainable growth that allows us to keep our down-to-earth orientation.

We put the same high quality into every product we offer, translating the best of current research into practical, accessible, easy-to-use materials. In this way we can create the best possible resources to help our customers teach about stress management and wellness promotion.

We also strive to treat our customers as we would like to be treated. If we fall short of our goals in any way, please let us know.

ABOUT OUR EMPLOYEES

Speaking of down-to-earth, that's a requirement for each and every one of our employees. We're all product consultants, which means that anyone who answers the phone can probably answer your questions (if they can't, they'll find someone who can.)

We focus on helping you find the products that fit your needs. And we've found that the best way to do that is to hire friendly and resourceful people.

ABOUT OUR ASSOCIATES

Who are the "associates" in Whole Person Associates? They're the trainers, authors, musicians, and others who have developed much of the material you see on these pages. We're always on the lookout for high-quality products that reflect our "whole person" philosophy and fill a need for our customers.

Most of our products were developed by experts who are the tops in their fields, and we're very proud to be associated with them.

ABOUT OUR CUSTOMERS

Finally, we wouldn't have a reason to exist without you, our customers. We've met some of you, and we've talked to many more of you on the phone. We are always aware that without you, there would be no Whole Person Associates.

That's why we'd love to hear from you! Let us know what you think of our products—how you use them in your work, what additional products you'd like to see, and what shortcomings you've noted. Write us or call on our toll-free line. We look forward to hearing from you!

©1994 Whole Person Press 210 W Michigan Duluth MN 55802   (800) 247-6789